C000261735

ONE HUNDRED
LAKE DISTRICT HILL WALKS

Gordon Brown

Photographs by Bill Stainton

Copyright ©, Gordon Brown and William Stainton, 1994

All Rights Reserved. No part of this publication may be reproduced, stored in a retrieval system, or transmitted in any form or by any means – electronic, mechanical, photocopying, recording, or otherwise – without prior written permission from the publisher.

Published by Sigma Leisure – an imprint of
Sigma Press, 1 South Oak Lane, Wilmslow, Cheshire SK9 6AR, England.

British Library Cataloguing in Publication Data
A CIP record for this book is available from the British Library.

ISBN: 1-85058-345-5

Typesetting and Design by: Sigma Press, Wilmslow, Cheshire.

Cover Picture: Scafell (Bill Stainton)

Cover Design: The Agency, Wilmslow

Printed by: Manchester Free Press

GENERAL DISCLAIMER: While every care has been taken in researching, writing and publishing this book, neither the author nor the publishers can accept any responsibility for any loss or injury to readers, however sustained.

Preface

This book is the fulfilment of my ambition to cover almost every peak in the Lake District National Park, an area of 800 square miles. With the help of this book, you should be able to enjoy your walks in the Lake District hills and mountains, as many have a right to be called, or over the fells as Cumbrians like their hill country to be known.

For the convenience of the walker, the book is in four sections, each coinciding with one of the four sheets of the Ordnance Survey Outdoor Leisure Series for the English Lakes: North Western, North Eastern, South Western and South Eastern. There are 25 walks based on each sheet and the result is intended to be a practical guide to be used both when planning walks and when on the hills.

One of the appeals of hill walking is the solitude; getting away from the bustle of town life. You can certainly do that in the Lake District National Park, where the rights of way are well-maintained and well-signposted by the Lake District Special Planning Board. As well as major peaks, all of the main Lakes are within easy striking distance of the routes.

Most of the walks are geared to car use, as public transport in the Lake District is infrequent and even non-existent in some areas. As will be seen, some of the rambles can be reached by public transport. Timetable details may be obtained from Cumberland Motor Services [Whitehaven (0946) 63222], Mountain Goat Lake District Mini-Bus Service [Windermere (05394) 45161] and British Rail [Carlisle (0228) 44711].

I have written all the walks and other articles in the book with the exception of walks 32 to 50, which are by Stuart Burgess, and walks 52 to 56 and 76 to 79, which are by John Nicholson. Stuart has walked extensively in Britain and is the author of a privately published long distance walk, "The West Lakes Way", between Whitehaven and Millom. John is an assistant editor of the *Cumberland Evening News & Star*,

Cumberland News and West Cumbria Evening News & Star in which he writes a weekly article, 'Mountain View Point'.

Bill Stainton, the photographer, is a retired nuclear worker who combines walking with camera work to produce fine pictures which he uses in slide shows, magazines and newspapers and which have been reproduced on postcards and calendars.

Gordon Brown

Acknowledgements and Dedication

The author wishes to acknowledge the valuable help of the following people:

Martin Hughes, for help in preparing draft sketch maps for the artist who produced the finished products.

Alec Robertson, for help with metric conversions.

Alan Taylor for permission to reproduce a list of Lake District mountains from a book written by his late father, Roland Taylor.

This book is dedicated to the neighbours, Monkwray Cottages. Kells, Whitehaven, for their help to the author with more than just a cup of tea during preparation of the book.

Contents

Introductory Notes

The North West

The South West

The North East

The South East

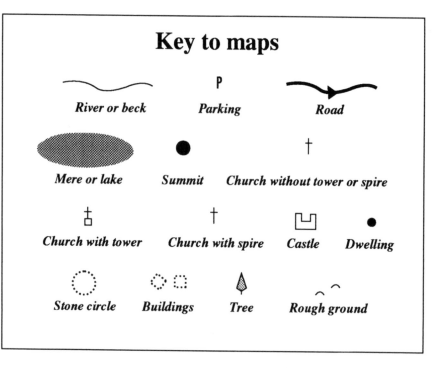

Key to maps

River or beck   P   *Road*

      Parking

Mere or lake   *Summit*   *Church without tower or spire*

Church with tower   *Church with spire*   *Castle*   *Dwelling*

Stone circle   *Buildings*   *Tree*   *Rough ground*

Introductory Notes

Before you set off: ten points to remember

1. The sketch maps are to give a quick, visual idea of each walk. They are not to a strict scale and they do not replace Ordnance Survey maps; the walks are based on the four sections of the 'English Lakes 1:25,000 Outdoor Leisure' Series, and the appropriate map should always be carried when walking in the Lake District.

2. The walking distance includes an allowance for the continuous variations from the route as it would be measured on the map. It is always necessary on a hill walk to make short detours to avoid bog, rocks, hillocks, etc. While an allowance has been made for this, the resultant figure must be approximate.

3. The amount of climbing given with each walk description is the sum of all the uphill sections of the route, from sea level.

4. Distances given within the texts are approximations for guidance only.

5. Compass directions and bearings given in the text are based on Ordnance Survey Grid North. After setting the compass to the map, the magnetic variation given at the top of OS maps must be added to the setting of the compass to get a true bearing.

6. Conditions in the countryside change as new forests are planted, fences erected, new roads laid over agricultural land and so on, so the passage of time may cause variations from the text. These, however, should not prevent you from finding a way round them.

7. Do not be tempted to tackle a challenging hill walk in bad weather. Ring Weatherline for the Lake District forecast (including conditions on the fells from the National Park ranger service) on 0768 - 775757 or Weathercall, for the general Cumbria forecast, on 0891 - 505319.

8. Walk within your ability. For this reason, a few of the walks in this book are not long and not entirely on hills, but are of the type which hillwalkers can still enjoy, perhaps on "rest" days or in inclement weather, or with the family.

9. Walk at your own pace. A reasonable estimate of walking time for an adult is 12 minutes for each kilometre plus a minute for each 10 metres of altitude climbed. Allow a 10 minute rest stop for each hour of walking.

10. Drink stream or beck water only from its highest point.

Cat Bells, a view seen on the first walk in this book

Playing Safe

The following is based on advice given by the British Mountaineering Council:

Select equipment after asking advice and learn how to use it – have a knowledge of basic First Aid – know how to navigate properly – attain a standard of physical fitness suited to your ambition – follow the Country Code.

It is wise always to carry waterproofs, spare sweater, map, compass, whistle and some food, with chocolate or other sugar-based confectionery, and a polythene survival bag for emergencies. In winter, increase clothing and food and carry a good torch, mitts and balaclava.

Make sure the expedition or climb you are planning is not beyond your training, experience or fitness. Stay on known routes until you have a good knowledge of an area, or become proficient in route-finding skills.

For the inexperienced, travelling alone is inadvisable. It is sound practice to leave word of your route and report your return. Check the local weather forecast before you leave your valley base.

Only venture onto snow and ice when you have fully mastered the use of ice axe and crampons.

In the event of injury, carry out immediate First Aid and evacuate the casualty or erect a shelter. Signal your distress, other mountaineers may be nearby and able to assist. Or, if appropriate, dial 999 and ask for Mountain Rescue assistance. The International Mountain Distress Signal is six rapid signals (by whistle, torch, shout, etc) repeated at one minute intervals until you are located.

Hints and Tips for a Great Day on the Fells

❏ Make sure your rucksack is not too heavy to carry for the walk.

❏ Take sufficient food, including fruit and chocolate. Nuts (with raisins or whatever else take your fancy) make a satisfying snack.

❏ Pack a first-aid kit with minimum requirements of plasters, bandages, antiseptic and treatment for insect stings (e.g. 'Wasp-eze') to deal with minor emergencies.

❑ Take with you (and know how to use) a compass, pedometer and map for the area. A notebook, pen and pencil can come in useful.

❑ Wear strong, comfortable boots and cotton socks under woollen ones.

❑ Take a warm jumper for when the weather cools. Wear a woollen hat in winter and a sun hat on hot, sunny days (they do happen!).

❑ Choice of other clothing is common sense and comfort. Shorts give you freedom in spring, summer and autumn, but corduroy trousers or breeches are recommended for the winter. Jeans or narrow trousers impede leg comfort for walking or climbing.

❑ Carry a torch with a good beam and spare batteries and bulbs.

❑ Take a whistle to summon help. (see previous page).

The Country Code

All users of the mountains should observe the Country Code, which runs:

❑ Guard against all risk of fire.

❑ Fasten all gates, unless you know that the farmer has left them open.

❑ Keep dogs under proper control.

❑ Keep to the paths across farm land.

❑ Avoid damaging fences, hedges and walls.

❑ Leave no litter

❑ Safeguard water supplies.

❑ Protect wild life, wild plants and trees.

❑ Go carefully on country roads

❑ Respect the life of the countryside

The North West

This is covered by the North West Sheet of the English Lakes Outdoor Leisure map.

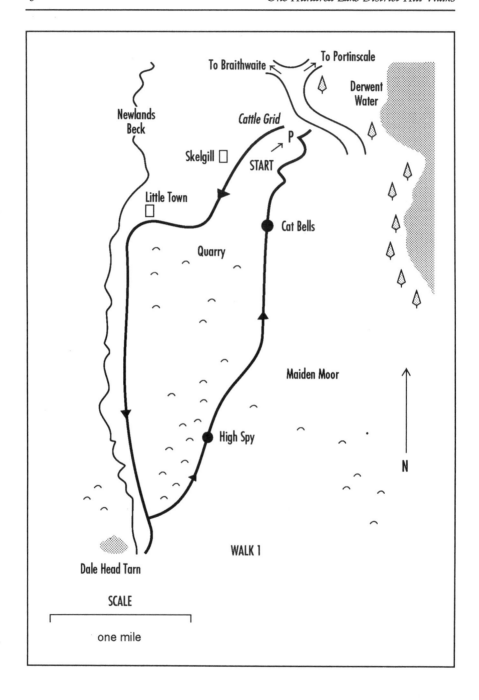

To Braithwaite

To Portinscale

Derwent Water

Newlands Beck

Cattle Grid

P

Skelgill

START

Little Town

Cat Bells

Quarry

Maiden Moor

High Spy

N

WALK 1

Dale Head Tarn

SCALE

one mile

1. High Spy and Cat Bells

A circular walk with fine views of Derwent Water and the Newlands Valley with chance for a lunch stop at Dale Head Tarn.

Walking distance: 13.6 ml/22km

Amount of climbing: 2112ft/650m

How to get there:

By car. Park near a cattle grid (MR247212) on the Swinside to Grange road, not far from Hawes End.

By bus: Mountain Goat, Keswick-Buttermere to and from Braithwaite.

Refreshments: Braithwaite (hotels and café).

Nearest tourist information: Moot Hall, Market Square, Keswick. Telephone (07687) 72645.

Follow the track past Gutherscale to Skelgill. Just short of a farm gate, go up left at a footpath sign. The broad track rises above the Newlands Valley. The path winds round an old quarry and over a beck and drops at the back of 17th century Newlands Church and white dwellings. Continue on the grass where the stone track bends right to a seat. Your track also becomes stony as you pass a stone barn bearing what appears to be a photograph of a Victorian lady, if not the Queen herself! Where a track comes down from the left, keep parallel with a beck.

The path narrows up the hill side and crosses a beck. Soon you reach a waterfall and go right on a south-east bearing. At the top of this ridge, go right again. Ignore the path coming in from the left.

Over a beck, arrive at a sheep pen near Dale Head Tarn, a pleasant place to dine. Retrace your steps across Newlands Beck and follow the path and cairns over High Spy (2143ft/653m), Maiden Moor and Cat Bells (1481ft/451m) to enjoy wonderful glimpses of Derwent Water to the right.

Follow north and north-east bearings before dropping on a zig-zag path to Skelgill Farm bed and breakfast sign. From here, you should be able to locate the parking spot. It is not possible to shorten the walk.

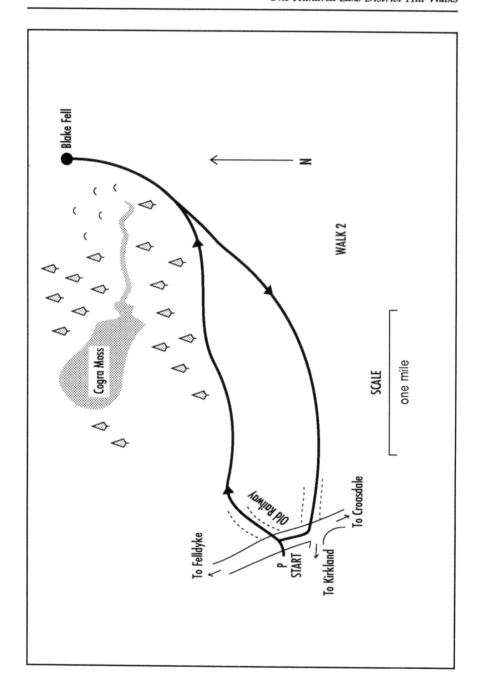

Blake Fell

Cogra Moss

N

WALK 2

SCALE

one mile

Old Railway

To Felldyke

To Croasdale

P
START

To Kirkland

2. Blake Fell

Iron ore mining was a thriving industry in West Cumbria in the 18th and 19th centuries and early this century. This ramble to the top of Blake Fell follows the footsteps of miners who earned their daily bread in such a mine at Kelton Head.

Walking distance: 4.5ml/7.2km

Amount of climbing: 893ft/275m

How to get there:

By car: Park on the Croasdale – Felldyke road (MR087183).

By bus: Whitehaven – Crossgates service to and from Kirkland (MR070179).

Refreshments: Inglenook Caravan park (MR 084205); The Tip public house (MR 076082); Ennerdale Bridge (MR 070159).

Nearest tourist information: Whitehaven Market Hall. Telephone (0946) 695678.

Facing Felldyke, take the right-hand stile and continue on the old mineral railway line that carried trucks to and from the mine. Over the second stile, cross a wire fence and keep in the same direction to go through a gate and reach the plantation corner. Here the path forks. Follow the right-hand grassy path and start a steady climb in three tiers before Blake Fell (1878ft/573m) is finally conquered.

At the top of the second rise is a glimpse of a majestic expanse of water known as Cogra Moss, lying below. To the right, Ennerdale Water comes into view.

Climb by the side of a wire fence before a stone structure shaped in a half-moon is reached on Blake's summit. Retrace your steps as far as the second stile going down in the wire fence and branch off diagonally left (west) across a moor. Eventually, run onto a track leading through a couple of gates to a point opposite a lane leading to the hamlet of Kirkland. Turn right for the car.

This is a walk to be commended more for its height than its mileage. The mineral railway ran for 3.5ml/5.6km from the Distington-Rowrah line to

Kelton Head and Knock Murton, a neighbouring fell in the mining area. It is not possible to shorten the walk.

Blake Fell is the highest peak in this group

3. Angler's Crag and Brown How

An undulating walk encircling the 2.5ml/4km long Ennerdale Water.

Walking distance: 7ml/11.2km

Amount of climbing: 1220ft/381m

How to get there:

By car. Bleach Green car park (MR85155).

Refreshments: Ennerdale Bridge (MR070159).

Nearest tourist information: See Walk 2.

Leaving the car park, turn left and pass over a bridge. The path swings right through a gate. Keep to the water's edge, passing through a wicket gate. Along the craggy path, in line with a white farmhouse across the lake, scramble up the fell-side a few yards to another path running parallel with the water.

A steady climb puts you on Angler's Crag (1000ft/300m). There is a flat bit before a few more uphill yards and a left bend. After another brief climb turn right along the cliff edge to a craggy summit on the slopes of Crag Fell. A right-hand path takes you to where the lake curves from behind Angler's Crag. Drop left to return to the lakeside path and a right turn. At the end of the lake, a ladder stile puts you on your way over the River Liza to the forestry road.

Left and first right, enter trees. After about 450ft/150m, start a right-hand climb to reach seats and viewpoint. From the notice board make up the fell-side, bending left in trees. Follow red topped posts and traverse flat stones near a post bearing a yellow "6". A flat stretch is followed by another short climb and a further notice board.

The path follows the trees left at an arrow. After a notice board about medieval dwellings, go right on a broad forestry track over Smithy Beck Bridge. Bend right where a left-hand track comes in.

Take a stony, uphill path on the right. On at cross-tracks, go over a fence stile next to a gate. Continue uphill near forest on Brown How (1060ft/

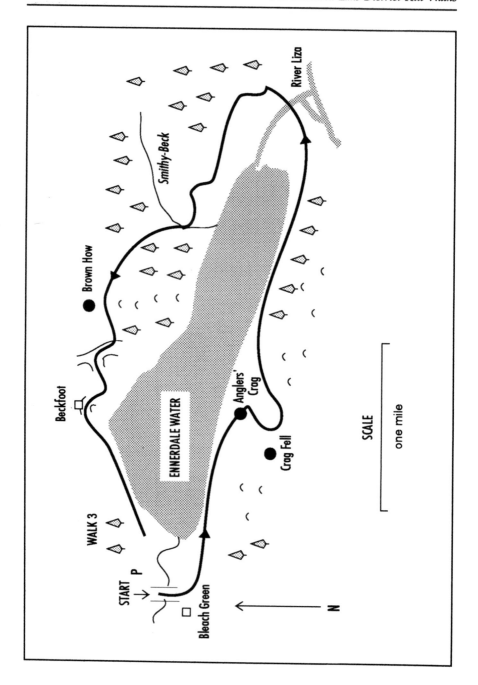

320m). Over crags and by a fenceside, negotiate a downhill, grassy slope and reach the road at Black Sail and Ennerdale National Trust signs. Turn right and take the first lane left. On the nearside of the white house, Beckfoot, go down to the lake, the perimeter path of which you follow right back to the car park.

Ennerdale from the Angler's Crag path

You may return to your car after coming off Angler's Crag (saving three miles) or crossing River Liza, following the lakeside path (saving two miles).

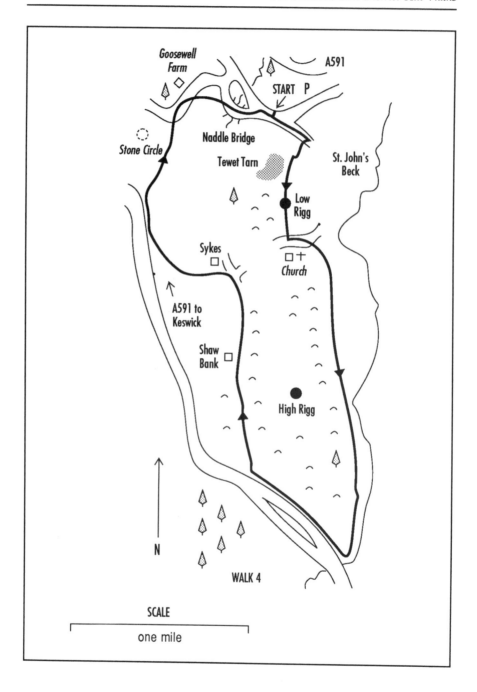

Goosewell
Farm

A591

START P

Stone Circle

Naddle Bridge

Tewet Tarn

St. John's
Beck

Low
Rigg

Sykes

Church

A591 to
Keswick

Shaw
Bank

High Rigg

N

WALK 4

SCALE

one mile

4. High Rigg and Low Rigg

A light, family walk taking in junior slopes. Ideal for winter.

Walking distance: 7.5ml/12km

Amount of climbing: 1127ft/347m

How to get there:

By car. Park along the lane signed to Burns about 1ml/1.5km off the A6(T) on left opposite Naddle Bridge Lane (MR303239).

By bus: Keswick-Threlkeld-Penrith service to and from Burns Road Ends.

Refreshments: Keswick and Threlkeld (MR325253).

Nearest tourist information: See Walk 1.

From the parking place, continue along the road to the first turn right signed to St John's Diocesan Centre. A couple of hundred yards on the right, take the path passing Tewet Tarn over Low Rigg to a stile opposite St John's in the Vale Church, a delightful mid-19th century fell church with features from an earlier edifice. Turn left and go through the first gate on the right on the bridleway for St John's Beck to a T-junction of grassy paths at a stone wall. Turn right with the beck to the left. Through another gate, the rock-strewn way rises above the beck on the lower slopes of High Rigg to reach the A591 Keswick to Windermere road.

Turn right. At the end of the dual-carriageway enter the growth a few yards on to embark on a footpath in the trees marked "Keswick". The path reaches a main path where the way is right. Now over the shoulder of High Rigg, move on a compass bearing of 340 degrees. Just short of Sykes, turn left on a footpath which is a continuation of the lane from St John's in the Vale Church. Go right on a two-way footpath sign in the middle of the field for the A591 road again.

Go right for 50 yards to a right turn on the Low Nest track. Over a cattle grid, go left, surmounting a stile. Diagonally to the trees and right through a gate, continue along a tarmac lane for the path to Castlerigg Stone Circle, dating from between 500 and 1300 BC. Returning to the same lane, go right as far as Goosewell Farm. Opposite is a path to Naddle bridge. A right turn leads to the Burns road opposite the parking space.

A glimpse across Tewett Tarn to Blencathra

5. Skiddaw

Skiddaw is the fourth highest mountain in the Lake district and England. This walk reaches the summit via the path from near Millbeck and returns to Keswick down what is popularly known as the Tourist Route.

Walking distance: 8.8ml/14.1km

Amount of climbing: 2808ft/864m

How to get there:

By car. There is plenty of car parking space in Keswick. However, the most convenient park to use for this walk is the Central, situated behind the north side of Market Street (MR267235). On entering the town from the A66 follow a road left from the mouth of Market Street to reach the car park on the right.

By bus: Whitehaven-Keswick service to Millbeck Lane Ends (MR253257).

Refreshments: Keswick

Nearest tourist information: See Walk 1

Motorists should walk back past the bus station entrance road and Pencil Museum. Cross the River Derwent bridge and take the left-hand riverside path which soon crosses fields to emerge at Stormwater Bridge. Turn right across the B5289 past Crosthwaite Church.

The path continues over a footbridge to cross the A66 and A591 roads to follow the mapped route of the Allerdale Ramble long distance footpath to Applethwaite. The first land on the left, behind Croft Head Farm puts you on a path running parallel with the Applethwaite-Millbeck minor road.

At Millbeck, where bus passengers pick up the walk (motorists may catch a bus at the bus station if not wishing to follow the above directions), turns on lanes to the right and left lead to a right-hand track. A few yards along is a Skiddaw footpath sign (MR257262) and the start of the climb.

At Carlside Tarn, there are, in fact, three small tarns. Here, take an east bearing (right) to a path which joins the Tourist Route to Skiddaw Man summit. Go left to reach the goal, the top of Skiddaw (3053ft/931m), with trig point, viewfinder and shelter. Retrace steps along the Tourist

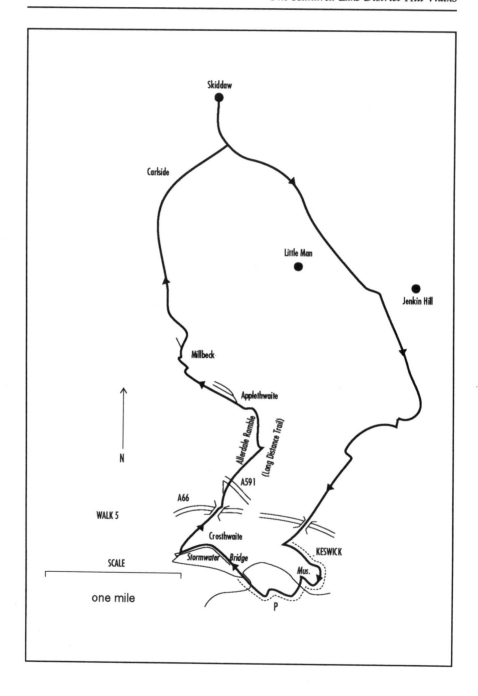

Route heading 100 degrees south-east over Little Man, and Jenkin Hill. Right through a car park at the foot for a few yards and through a left-hand wicket gate under trees to cross road bridge to Spooney Green Lane junction (signed). Go left and along Brandlesholme Road, left at a round-about near a leisure pool and under a railway bridge. The road bends left at a park corner near a museum. Go right at the cross-roads to the car park, continuing along the road to the bus station if travelling by bus.

Skiddaw from Derwent Water

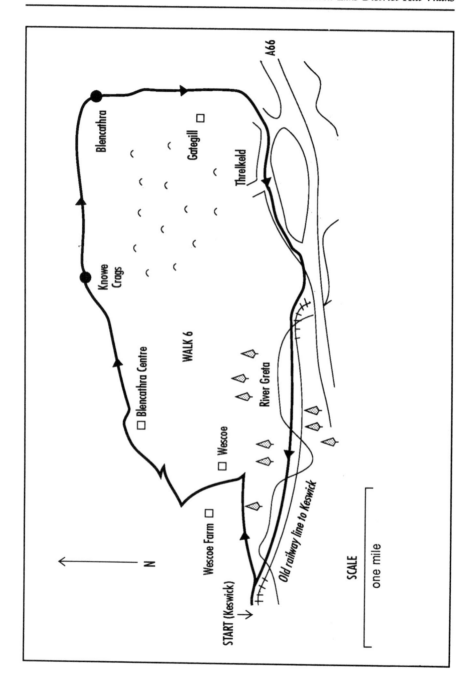

6. Blencathra

A delightful walk along the bed of a disused railway line leads to a demanding climb to the top of the thirteenth highest peak in the Lake District.

Walking distance: 10.6ml/17.1km

Amount of climbing: 2398ft/738m

How to get there:

By car. Park in any car park in Keswick and go along Station Street. Cross the main road by the side of Fitz Park and continue ahead to a point near the former Keswick Railway Station and a bridge (MR272237).

By bus: Buses to Keswick from Carlisle; Penrith; Lancaster (via Kendal), Windermere, Ambleside and Grasmere; Whitehaven (via Cockermouth and Workington). See CMS timetable.

Refreshments: Keswick and Threlkeld.

Nearest tourist information: See Walk 1.

Just under the bridge, climb the steps on the right. A left turn starts you on the line of the former Penrith-Cockermouth railway, opened in 1864 and closed in the early 1970s. Follow an easterly direction.

After passing under the A66 road, the path crosses the River Greta three times before you turn off through a small gate on the left just short of the fourth bridge. Cross a footbridge; then a stone bridge on the uphill lane to Wescoe. At a T-junction, go left on a cul-de-sac sign. Past Wescoe Farm, follow the first footpath sign on the right. Follow the signs into the Blencathra Outdoor Centre, formerly a sanatorium.

Right at the end of buildings near a car park are signs for Skiddaw House (a youth hostel) and Blencathra. Take the left fork behind further buildings. Turn left at the top on Bassenthwaite and Skiddaw House sign and begin the climb to Blencathra summit (2847ft/868m) at a step-stile up a right-hand slope.

One path runs into another as you continue climbing over a variable surface across Knowe Crags and several pinnacles before reaching the goal, also mapped as Saddleback. Keep ahead at the top down the precarious-looking Hall's Fell Ridge to Threlkeld. Reach a "No cycling or horses" notice and ford a beck. Keep it on the left to a small gate and seat. Drop through another small gate into a farmyard, Gategill (MR325261). Make through Threlkeld to MR315248 to rejoin the old railway back to Keswick.

A glimpse of Thirlmere with Blencathra in the background

7. Rannerdale Knotts

The sloping approaches to Rannerdale Knotts have a superb display of bluebells in season. It is arguably the finest in the Lake District and attributable, legend has it, to the richness of the soil. The soil was enriched, the story goes, by the blood of the Normans, defeated in battle here. Superb views of Crummock Water and Buttermere. Ideal for a fine evening.

Walking distance: 3.2ml/5.2km

Amount of climbing: 812ft/250m

How to get there:

By car: Cinderdale Common car park (MR162194) on the B5289 north of Buttermere village.

By bus: Mountain Goat, Keswick-Buttermere service. Follow map between Buttermere and Cinderdale Common car park.

Refreshments: Buttermere (see Walk 15).

Nearest tourist information: See Walk 1.

Head south on a well-trodden path to the right-hand ladder stile, from where the path goes left to disappear onto the fells. Referring to the map, you will find that High Rannerdale is on the left as Squat Beck is followed to a T-junction of ways.

Successive right turns within a short distance start you on the trek over Rannerdale Knotts and switch you from a valley walk to a hill climb. After surmounting Low Bank (984ft/300m), you reach cairns, the second of which marks Rannerdale Knotts summit (1164ft/355m). Crummock and Buttermere are now seen in all their glory.

The way down towards Crummock, the right-hand of the two "lakes" to the left as you face north, is tricky. The path is clear but broken with scree and boulders with "safety" grass thrown in for good measure. Reaching the B5289 road, turn left for Buttermere and, for the car, go right to pass Rannerdale Farm and cross Rannerdale Bridge back to the right-hand car park.

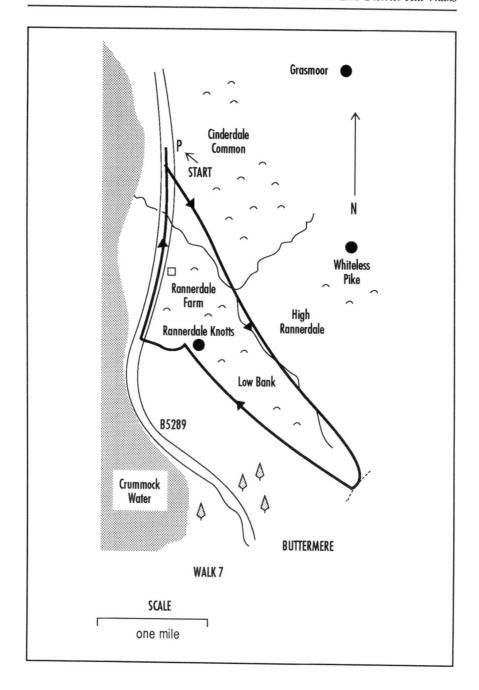

Grasmoor

Cinderdale
Common

P
START

N

Whiteless
Pike

Rannerdale
Farm

High
Rannerdale

Rannerdale Knotts

Low Bank

B5289

Crummock
Water

BUTTERMERE

WALK 7

SCALE

one mile

Rannerdale Knotts are at the centre of this picture

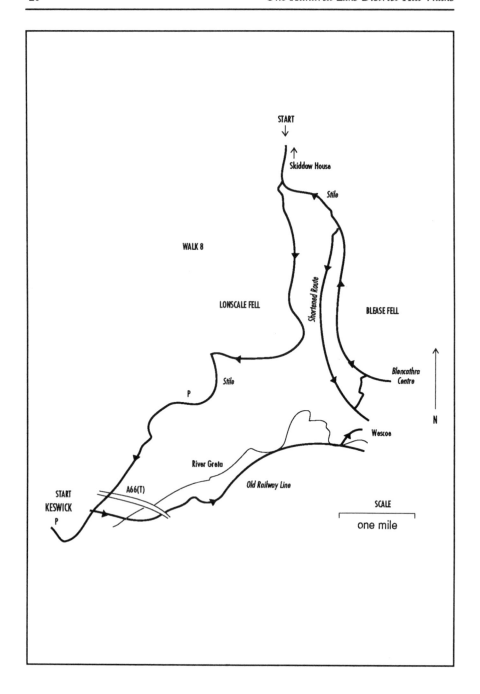

START
↓
↑
Skiddaw House

Stile

WALK 8

LONSCALE FELL

Shortened Route

BLEASE FELL

Blencathra
Centre

Stile

P

N

Wescoe

River Greta

Old Railway Line

START
KESWICK
P

A66(T)

SCALE

one mile

8. Blease and Lonscale Fells

This superb walk starts from Keswick, but visits less-frequented fells. The first part of the route is ahred with Walk 6.

Walking distance: 10ml/16km

Amount of climbing:1148ft/350m

How to get there:

By car: Park in Keswick, see Walk 6

By bus: See Walk 6

Refreshments: Keswick and Threlkeld

Nearest tourist information: See Walk 1.

Follow the route for Blencathra Outdoor Centre as described in Walk 6. Instead of turning off on MR303256 for the ascent of Blencathra, continue along the track beyond the car park.

After about two kilometres, ford Roughten Gill below a waterfall and less than a kilometre on, ford more water; the track bends left just short of a sheepfold before going over a couple of footbridges and a ladder stile. Over another beck, it is but a few yards to a T-junction of tracks at what is marked on the map as Guide Stone (MR293279). If you are seeking accommodation you may turn right here for Skiddaw House Youth Hostel.

The way of the walk, however, is left on an undulating path looking across the Glenderaterra Valley to the path you have left. Over a footbridge, the way is wet, stony and rising. After crossing rocks, the path goes "green" before going over a step stile at the side of a gate.

Heading in the direction of the attractive view of Derwent Water, follow the path over Whitbeck and then head left. Go through a wicket gate near a large gate, then join the track known as the Tourist Route to and from Skiddaw. Between a wire fence and a stone wall, the path reaches a car park (MR281253) mentioned in Walk 5. From this point follow the directions in Walk 5 for the return to Keswick.

To shorten the walk by about a mile, take the path at MR298273 which leaves the main track from the back of the Blencathra Centre just short of Roughten Gill. At Wescoe, retrace steps along the old railway line to Keswick.

Blencathra and Lonscale Fell

9. Lorton Fells

A pleasant climb taking in Spout Force waterfall, beck and forestry. The walk is off Whinlatter Pass, which has a Visitor Centre, over a range of hills known as the Lorton Fells.

Walking distance: 5ml/8km

Amount of climbing: 1787ft/550m

How to get there:

By car. Parking space near a disused quarry at Scawgill Bridge (MR177258)

Refreshments: Lorton and Cockermouth

Nearest tourist information: Lorton Post Office and Riverside car park, Market Street, Cockermouth. Telephone: (0900) 822634

Follow the wooden footpath sign through a green wicket gate alongside Blaze Beck. After 200 yards, pass through another wicket gate, continuing to Spout Force waterfall, which is signposted. From the viewpoint retrace steps a few yards and take the right-hand fork uphill through trees.

Zig-zagging with the waterfall to the right, find yellow line markers for a nature trail and reach a clearing. Go right on the forestry road over a bridge. The road ahead goes left. After a few hundred yards cross a left-hand stile at the side of a padlocked gate. Climb the path which crosses Aiken Beck at the side of the plantation you have just left and is now on the left.

The path winds north to the foot of Todd Fell topped with a rocky knob, where there are several faint paths. Take the near right-hand one cutting back. Follow the distinct path which soon swings round to north (40 degrees) heading towards the cairn of Broom Fell.

Across a depression, the path rises again on north (40 degrees). Cross a path to limestone outcrops and reach the tall cairn on the summit of Broom Fell, crossing the fence stile on the far side to take in the view of Bassenthwaite Lake to the left. Follow this path eastwards. Aim for the part of the cartrack that can be seen on the hill ahead. Just over this, go right at an iron post in the ground and climb on a faint path over Lord's

Seat by an iron contraption. Cross a step stile on a well-made path through Beckstones Plantation. At marker post 5, go right and round a left-hand bend.

The broad track winds to the sign for Tarbarrel Moss. Here the way is to the right. Follow this, ignoring all other turns, past Darling How Farm to the road. A right turn for a few hundred yards takes you back to the car.

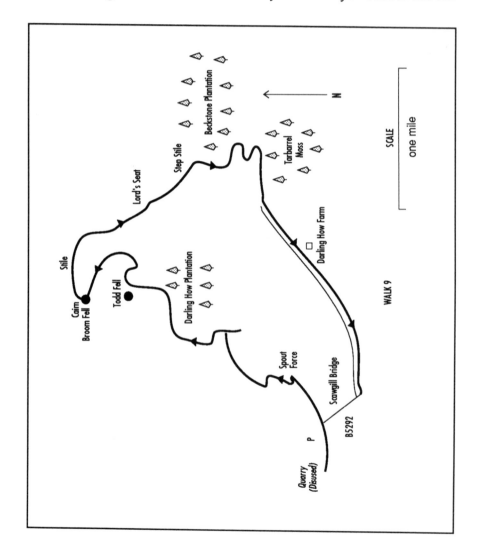

10. Grisedale Pike and Hopegill Head

A challenging walk with tricky rocks to negotiate on the ascents of Grisedale Pike and Hopegill Head.

Walking distance: 6.3ml/10.2km

Amount of climbing: 2372ft/730m

How to get there:

By car: Travel through Braithwaite village on the Whinlatter road to park in a clearing at a blue and white 'P ¹/₂ml" sign. This indicates further parking which may be used should the clearing be full (MR228237)

By bus: See Walk 1

Refreshments: See Walk 1

Nearest tourist information: See Walk 1

Into the clearing from the road take the Grisedale footpath sign up right-hand steps to start a steady climb over a stile and along a broad grassy track with fine views, for about 1.2ml/2km. The path skirts Kinn and a disused quarry over Sleet How to reach the climb to the summit of Grisedale Pike (2593ft/791m).

Immediately over the Pike, there is a drop and then a sudden rise up Hobcarton Crag to the summit of Hopegill Head (2525ft/770m). On the drop over the Head take the left fork of two paths at a cairn. The path goes down Sand Hill (2457ft/756m) to arrive at a cross-path on Coledale Hause with Eel Crag in front.

The way is left on a descent with High Force and Force Crag on the left. After a few metres, the working Force Crag Mine comes into view down to the left. Continue along the path to cross stepping stones at the ford over Coledale Beck to the right of the mine. This way, shown in black and white on the OS map, is a better way than that shown in green.

With the beck now on the right climb through the gorse to the quarry road and continue right on a flat way for 1.2ml/2km back to the car. Should you wish to go into Braithwaite for refreshment, a narrow right-hand path is signed just above the village.

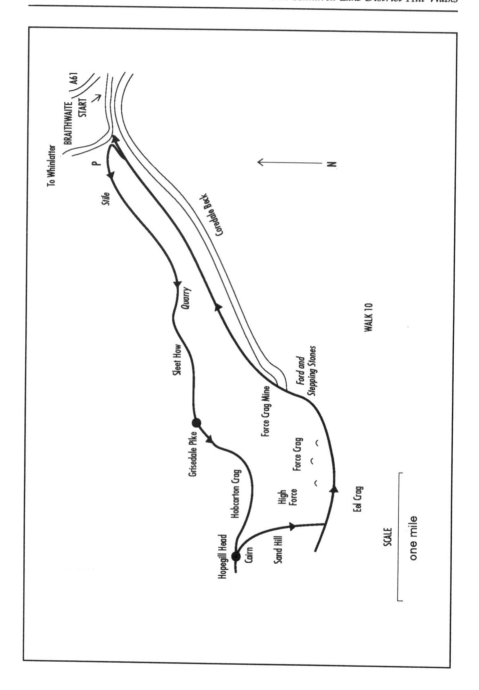

Across Derwent Water to Causey Pike (left) and Grisedale Pike (right)

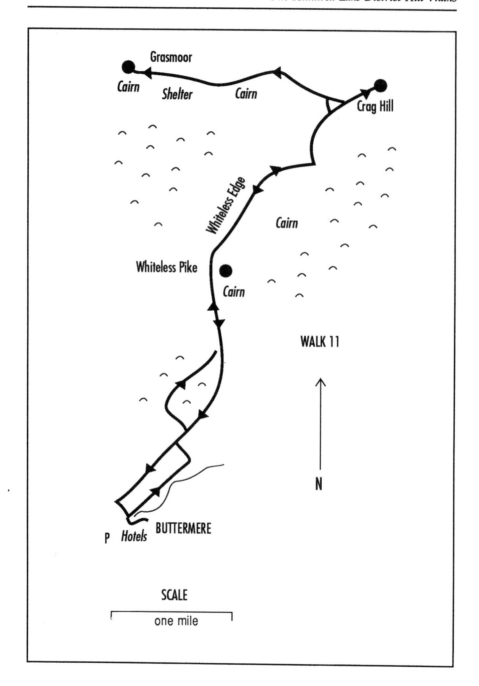

Grasmoor

Cairn   Shelter   Cairn

Crag Hill

Whiteless Edge

Whiteless Pike

Cairn

Cairn

WALK 11

N

BUTTERMERE

P   Hotels

SCALE

one mile

11. Whiteless Pike, Crag Hill and Grasmoor

A steady slog rewarded by breathtaking views of Buttermere, Crummock Water and Loweswater in one of the most popular areas of the Lake District.

Walking distance: 6.8ml/11km

Amount of climbing: 3220ft/991m

How to get there:

By car. Parking is at a premium. At the time of writing, double yellow lines littered the main lane through Buttermere. The public car park for this walk is near the Bridge and Fish Hotels (MR175169)

By bus: Mountain Goat Keswick-Buttermere services

Refreshments: Buttermere (see Walk 15)

Nearest tourist information: See Walk 1

Onto the road at the Bridge Hotel, cross the bridge spanning Mill Beck and turn immediately right on the Ghyll Wood sign. On the main path above the ghyll, fork left and after a few metres climb a left-hand wall ladder stile.

Cross a main track and take the one rising ahead towards the rocky escarpment of Whiteless Breast. Ignore the next path left but on reaching a second path, a broad greensward flanked by ferns, take it and go right at the next hillock.

Ignore the turn running parallel with Crummock Water at this stage and continue towards crags. Round a rock corner ignore the first turn left and continue on a stone and grass path. A triangle of paths comes in on the left. Take one of these and after a few yards fork right and go left on a sheep track. Fork right again soon afterwards.

Climb a narrow path over rocks on 160 degrees and continue up a grassy slope above Rowantree Beck to reach a main path, which you take left to the cairn on top of Whiteless Pike (2159ft/650m) and over Whiteless Edge to the main track between Crag Hill (2729ft/839m) and Grasmoor (2769ft/852m).

Crag Hill is to the right which I suggest you do first. Then come down again and carry on to the shelter on top of Grasmoor. To return to Buttermere, retrace your steps over Whiteless Pike and continue on this main route down to a small gate near a right-hand wall and the road, where a left turn for a few yards leads back to the hotels and car parks.

Grasmoor and Whiteless Pike from Mellbreak

12. Gasgale Gill and Whiteside

Stunning views of Loweswater and Crummock Water are the rewards for a steady climb up Gasgale Gill to vantage points for the ascent of Sand Hill, Hopegill Head and Whiteside.

Walking distance: 4.8ml/7.5km

Amount of climbing: 3152ft/970m

How to get there:

By car. Lanthwaite Green Farm roadside car park (MR158208) on the B5289 Cockermouth to Buttermere Road.

Refreshments: Buttermere, three miles south (see Walk 15)

Nearest tourist information: See Walk 9

Go left and take the signed path opposite the farm just over 100 yards short of a cattle grid. Cross Liza Beck at a convenient spot and keep the same direction along Gasgale Gill, steadily rising over sometimes precariously narrow and rock-strewn path to the first junction of paths at Coledale Hause.

Head left up Sand Hill, which rises immediately above Gasgale Gill. Climb to a cairn at the top, of Sand Hill, looking down at Loweswater. A depression followed by a 14-metre climb takes you to the summit of Hopegill Head. The way bends left along the ridge over Whiteside above Gasgale Crags. Looking down through space in the Gill, you get a wonderful glimpse of Crummock Water, which comes into full view along with Loweswater a few yards on, before you start to drop carefully down the scree and badly eroded path with a few safe havens of greenery, which is a better foothold, alongside Whiteside End and Boat Crag.

The car park is in view as a footbridge is approached, after a small tarn on the right of the path. Aim for white farm dwellings before the path winds left to the road and the car park a few yards to the left.

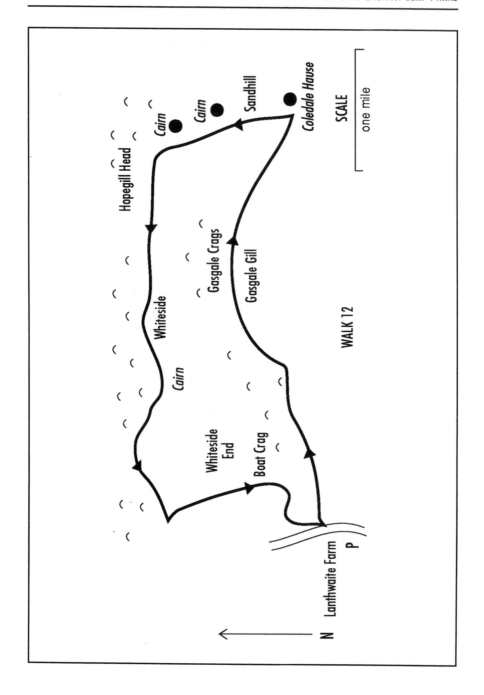

WALK 12

SCALE
one mile

13. Loweswater and Darling Fells

A leg-stretcher over junior slopes culminating in a testing 273 metres drop and a delightful half-round of Loweswater taking in Holme Wood.

Walking distance: 5ml/8km

Amount of climbing: 919ft/283m

How to get there:

By car. Parking space alongside a telephone kiosk (MR117223), not to be confused with the "P" marked on the OS map further along the Loweswater lake-side road.

Refreshments: Grange Country House Hotel (a few hundred yards from car park on the right of the road towards Mockerkin).

Nearest tourist information: See Walk 9

Opposite the car parking space, take the Mossergate bridleway. Gently rise, ignoring the Askill drive on the left, although this is marked ·in green on the map, and continue ahead through a gate. A left fork takes you through another gate.

Right at a cross-track, you are still parallel with Loweswater, until turning left on a broad lane. At a wayside seat dedicated to John W. Duff, who died in 1984, carry on a few yards to climb steps and over a double step stile on the Foulsyke sign.

Embark on a climb up Darling Fell (1290ft/391m), zig-zagging onto the shoulder at a right-hand fence, which you follow until finding a step stile. Over the stile, continue along the path still parallel with Loweswater, now offering a greater bird's eye view, to reach the summit of Loweswater Fell (not to be confused with a fell of the same name mapped to the south) at 1390ft/423m.

Crummock Water is in view ahead with Mellbreak towering above it. Now for a descent that illustrates the value of wire fences as hand-rails. Down 887ft/273m to Pottergill, turn right from the stile through the trees. The track winds left over a stile at the side of a gate at the end of the trees. Continue on the track at a further gate, passing a house to emerge on the road at Foulsyke. Go right and right again at the next

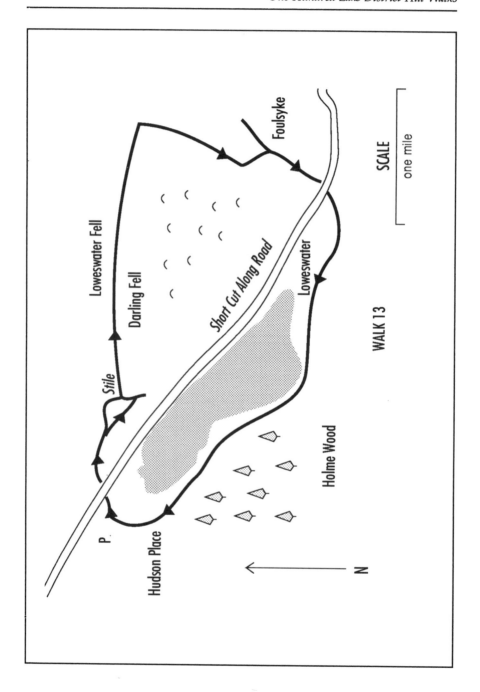

Foulsyke

Loweswater Fell

Darling Fell

Short Cut Along Road

Loweswater

Stile

P.

Hudson Place

Holme Wood

SCALE
one mile

WALK 13

N

road for about 100 yards. Left at the next bridleway sign, carry on through the National Trust car park, going left to start a lakeside walk through Holme Wood. Right at Hudson Place, take the right-hand step-stile over a meadow and footbridge before following left-hand hedge to the car park. You may shorten the walk by half a mile by using the road back to the car.

Mellbreak and Crummock Water, as seen from Darling Fell

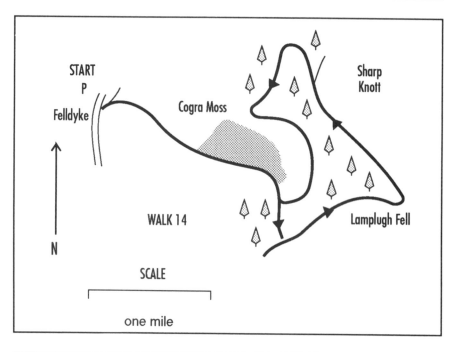

Across Ennerdale Water to Lamplugh Fells from Crag Fell

14. Lamplugh Fell and Cogra Moss

Lamplugh Fell is one of the lower slopes of the Western Lake District, but it provides a pleasant walk through forestry with a bird's eye view of an attractive stretch of fishing water known as Cogra Moss.

Walking distance: 4.4ml/7.1km

Amount of climbing: 422ft/130m

How to get there:

By car. Felldyke car park (MR83198)

By bus: Whitehaven-Crossgates (MR077210), then follow the OS map to Felldyke.

Refreshments: See Walk 2

Nearest tourist information: See Walk 2

Go along a narrow path out of the car park and up four steps, then turn left on a rough lane. After 10 yards go through a wicket gate marked "Footpath Cogra Moss".

At a further wicket gate at a memorial seat, for local artist, the late Ron Dickinson, enter trees with Cogra Moss on the left. Opposite the end of the lake, take the high path to reach a broad, red shale forestry track, on Lamplugh Fell (300m/975ft). Go left and soon you will get a great view of Cogra waters.

The track winds through the forestry peacefully. At a fork, take the broad, rocky road, stooping beneath Sharp Knott (1557ft/482m) bending leftwards and interchanging broad and narrow to soon run back to the banks of Cogra Moss, at the point where you took the high path on the outward journey. Retrace steps to the car.

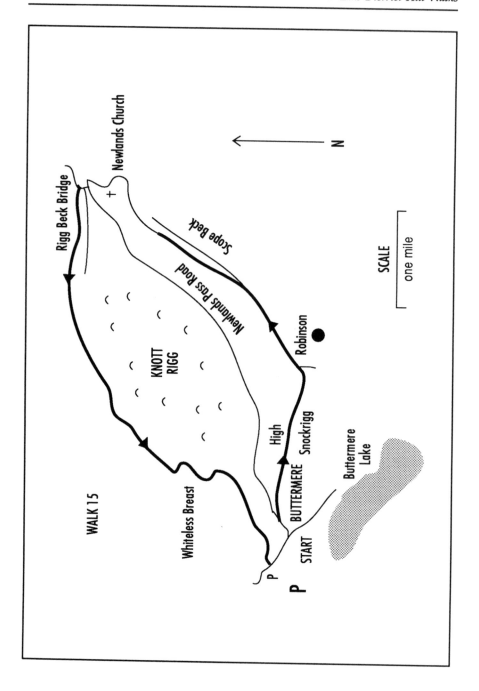

15. Robinson and the Derwent Fells

A moderate round from Buttermere goes over the outstanding peak of Robinson and crosses the Newlands Pass to finish on the lower slopes of the Derwent Fells.

Distance: 9.2ml/14km

Amount of climbing: 3250ft/1000m

How to get there:

By car: Park behind Fish and Bridge Hotels or in National Trust car park in Buttermere (MR176170).

By bus: Mountain Goat from Keswick.

Refreshments: Fish and Bridge Hotels; Farm café; Trevere guest house (cups of tea only).

Nearest tourist information: See Walk 1

From the village, take the Newlands Pass road on the far side of the church, where there is a memorial to lakeland fell walker and writer Alfred Wainwright, looking out of a window to his favourite Haystacks.

In a few hundred yards on the right go up a grassy track on a small wooden footpath sign. The path winds over High Snockrigg and Buttermere Moss.

Robinson (2417ft/373m) lies ahead. Head towards the summit on 120 degrees east, as there can be confusion with a maze of sheep tracks. On Robinson with Derwent Water in the distance, go left at a T-junction of tracks, following cairns and skirting Robinson Crags to eventually spot a dam down to the right and then follow the line of Scope Beck running from the dam.

On bearing of 20 degrees north, woods and a farmhouse are spotted before dropping through a gate. A dwelling is sandwiched between the next two gates before a National Trust sign is passed

Continue on a lane with the 17th century Newlands Church and 19th century school on the left. At a road junction turn left. Right at the next one on the Newlands Pass road reach a hairpin bend near a quarry clearing used as a car park. You have now arrived at Rigg Beck, the half-way stage where you could shorten the walk by catching a Mountain Goat bus to Buttermere or Keswick.

Continuing, from Rigg Beck Bridge, on the bend of the road, follow a sign pointing along the left-hand path parallel with the beck. It takes you over lower slopes of the Derwent Fells through Rigg Screes.

The path is narrow and the weather was wet with a facing head wind the day I went this way. The path bends left twice over a couple of fords and winds its way over the edge of Whiteless Breast to reach the B5289 Buttermere road near High House Crag. The NT car park is a few yards to the right. The village is to the left as you pass Trevere guest house, a good place for a welcome cup of tea.

The Newlands Pass, looking towards Grasmoor

16. Robinson and Hindscarth

The first three miles from Rigg Beck Bridge to Robinson summit is the reverse of part of the previous walk. The return from Hindscarth is on the opposite side of Scope Beck.

Distance: 7.5ml/12km

Amount of climbing: 2340ft/722m

How to get there:

By car. Park in quarry clearing, Rigg Beck (MR229201).

By bus: Mountain Goat between Keswick and Buttermere. Alight and re-board at Rigg Beck.

Refreshments: On the homeward journey at Low Snab Farm (tea and cake sign on gate) just before crossing Newlands Beck footbridge. Otherwise Buttermere or Keswick.

Nearest tourist information: See Walk 1

Uphill from the quarry clearing, take the left-hand turning to the land on the far side of the Grecian Villa-type building. After a few hundred yards, cross a bridge and follow the right-hand Newlands Church sign. Nearly a mile past the church there is a way to vary the walk by taking an uphill grassy path to keep parallel with the track to Robinson. This alternative route adds some excitement to the walk by crossing over the tricky rocks of High Snab Bank and Robinson Crags.

After, on average, a couple of hours of walking, Robinson (summit 2,417ft/737m) is reached. Keeping direction on a south bearing, a T-junction is reached with a track running in front of a fence. To the left is the way (opposite a stile in the fence) over Littledale Edge to a solitary iron post and, further left, turn on a 60 degrees north bearing over Hindscarth.

Just over the windy summit, there is a shelter and beyond there are many tricky crags to contend with on the long drop to Low Snab and the tantalising possibility of tea and cake, according to a notice on a farm gate. At the gate, the path winds right and then, over Newlands Beck

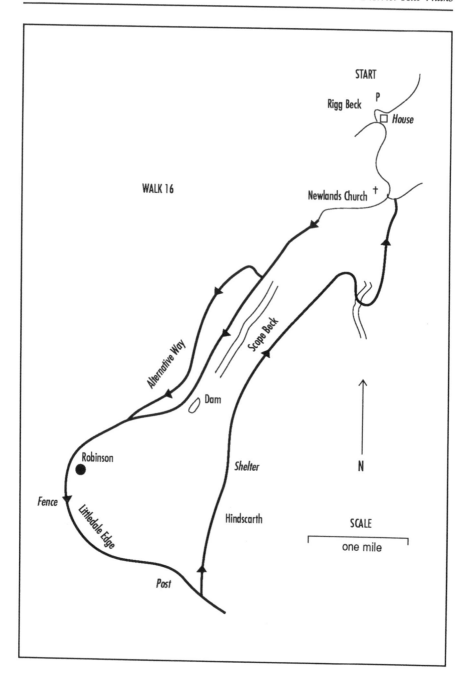

START

Rigg Beck   P

☐ House

WALK 16

Newlands Church   †

Scope Beck

Alternative Way

Dam

↑

N

Robinson

Shelter

Fence

Littledale Edge

Hindscarth

SCALE

one mile

Post

footbridge, to a broad track, where the way is left. After about a kilometre, a narrow left-hand path slides down to a lane near a car park and a left turn to retrace steps to Rigg Beck.

Robinson and Hindscarth

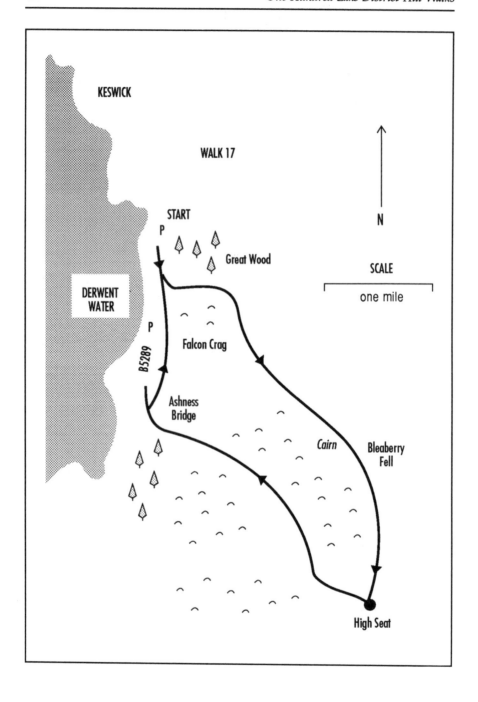

17. Bleaberry Fell and High Seat

A wonderful sub-2,000 feet walk over the roof of Keswick with commanding views of Derwent Water.

Distance: 5.5ml/8km

Amount of climbing: 1846ft/568m

How to get there:

By car. Great Wood car park (MR271212) on the Keswick-Borrowdale road (B5289).

By bus: Keswick-Seatoller service (CMS), to Great Wood.

Nearest tourist information: See Walk 1

Start in Great Wood car park and surmount the stile at the side of a gate on the Ashness Bridge and Walla Crag footpath. Rising before a footbridge, fork left up stone steps and through a small gate above Cat Gill. Another small gate puts you on a zig-zag uphill route, passing a left-hand wall style as you keep on a broad, grassy track.

At Cairn go sharp right on 165 degrees south. Arriving on a hillock, drop left to a sheepfold and head for the path which runs parallel on the far side of it (MR278300). The hillside is a mass of purple heather as you go right and then head across the moor to the big summit of Bleaberry Fell, diagonally left.

Bleaberry Fell is 1917ft/590m above sea level and from it a path leads to the unmistakeable High Seat (1976ft/608m above sea level) with its outstanding chimney-like trig point.

Make a descent on 290 degrees, dropping around 1,000 feet before rising to the summit of Dodd, then up and down over cairns and crags and zig-zagging towards Derwent Water in the distance.

Dropping through gorse and heather over a wall ladder stile, follow the left-hand fence side with a small waterfall and Barrow Beck on the right. Arrive opposite a car park and turn right on the lane over Ashness Bridge, about 10 yards over which follows a right-hand footpath sign marked Great Wood and Keswick. Under a ladder stile in the shadow of

Falcon Crag, go up by the side of a wall and then up steps over the footbridge where you forked left up steps on the outward journey.

Now keep straight on to retrace steps to the Great Wood car park.

Derwent Water from Walla Crag

18. Great Borne and Red Pike

Walking from desolation into a tourist trap in one ramble can be a familiar experience in the Lake District. So it is on scrambling up the National Trust path from Ennerdale to the summit of Great Borne (2019ft/616m) and then tramping over to the much more attractive Red Pike (2479ft/755m), usually raided by tourists who have stepped up from Buttermere.

Distance: 7.4ml/12.2km

Amount of climbing: 2551ft/785m

How to get there:

By car. Park in Bowness Knott car park (MR110153).

Refreshments: Ennerdale Bridge (MR070158). Also, Gillerthwaite Youth Hostel (coming off Red Pike) may serve a cup of tea.

Nearest tourist information: See Walk 2

About 500 metres from the car park in the Ennerdale Bridge direction, go over a right-hand fence at National Trust and bridleway signs. Starting from 120 feet above sea level, you are confronted with a steady climb of 496 feet on the top side of Rake Beck as the path zig-zags to a left fork which starts you on the second half of the ascent.

Soon an ancient fox trap is reached. This is a deep four-sided stone enclosure, no longer used the trapping of foxes. The only entry is at the top where a fox would follow a scent and be unable to get out.

You also enjoy a good view of the surrounding countryside from this point before reaching a shelter and trig point on Great Borne summit. To the north, Blake and Knockmurton fells can be seen before taking a 60 degrees bearing to a fence line, which you follow to the right. This is Copeland borough boundary.

The path leaves the fence to become a broad, grassy path over Starling Dodd (2057ft/633m) before dropping to the aptly named Little Dodd, which is 139ft/43m lower.

The cairn on top of Starling Dodd is made up of stones and old pieces of fencing. From this cairn continue east, following a broken fence line and then a winding path to the pinnacle of Red Pike.

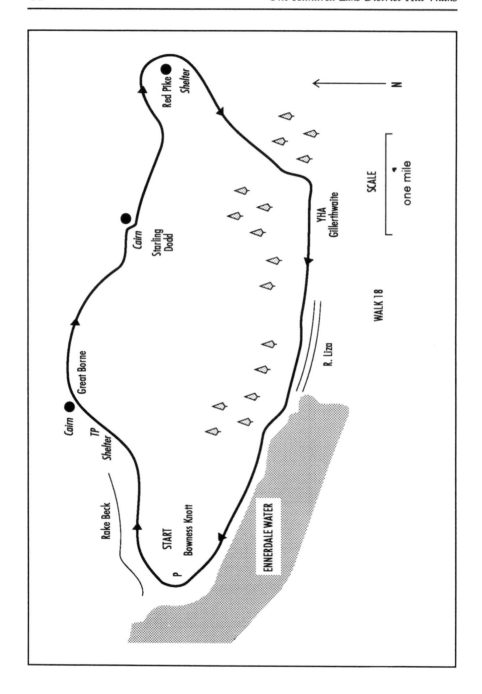

N

SCALE
one mile

WALK 18

Red Pike
Shelter

Starling
Dodd

Cairn

Great Borne

Cairn

TP

Shelter

Rake Beck

Bowness Knott

START

P

YHA
Gillerthwaite

R. Liza

ENNERDALE WATER

From here, the highest peak of the walk, can be seen four "lakes". It must be the best vantage point for lakes in the whole of Lakeland. To the west there is Ennerdale and from the other side of the shelter, in line from the left, Loweswater, Crummock Water and Buttermere.

A west bearing is taken for a few yards on leaving the shelter, then south to a broken fence line to go west again with Ennerdale Water ahead, slightly to the left.

It is an exhilarating 1985ft/611m drop down a well-worn path, zig-zagging its stony way to arrive at the side of a beck, which you cross before crossing another beck and continuing in the same direction over a fence stile between two plantations.

At a choice of three stiles at the cattle grid on the forestry road, turn right past Gillerthwaite Youth Hostel, the farm of outdoor author and broadcaster Bob Orrell and a field centre.

After a while continue off the forestry road along the River Liza path starting from the mouth of the broad forestry road coming in from the left. Back on the road at a picnic table, you just have a small climb over a hump in the road to find the car park on the right.

The fox trap on Great Borne

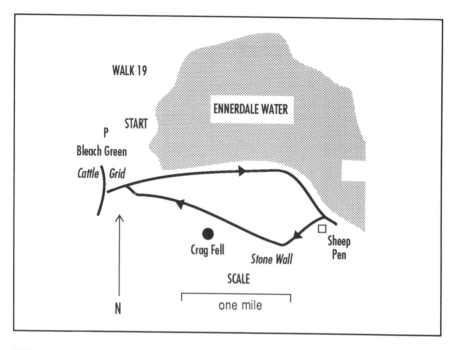

WALK 19

ENNERDALE WATER

START

P

Bleach Green

Cattle Grid

Crag Fell

Stone Wall

Sheep Pen

SCALE

one mile

N

Crag Fell, Ennerdale

19. Crag Fell

Another walk in and above the charming Ennerdale Valley and covering a little of the ground in Walk 3.

Distance: 3ml/4.2km

Amount of climbing: 1537ft/473m

How to get there:

By car: Park as for Walk 3

Refreshments: See Walk 3.

Nearest tourist information: See Walk 3.

From Bleach Green car park, over the River Ehen Bridge and keep ahead with Ennerdale Lake to the left and Bleach Green Cottages on the right. Along a broad track, go over Crag Farm cattle grid and at the farm gate keep the wire fence on the left. Over a ladder stile go left to surmount a fence stile at a beck and follow the famous Coast to Coast route along the lakeside.

After a few hundred yards the path starts rising above Ennerdale Lake and becomes undulating over crags. At a fork of paths, take the right-hand one before reaching a wall gap at a sheepfold. Climb along the near side of the wall. Reaching a sheep track, at a sheep tunnel in the wall, turn-right. Soon, the sheep track becomes stony and then grassy rising onto Crag Fell.

Looking down on the lake, the view is tremendous as you continue over challenging scree to meet paths to Crag Fell summit. Returning from the summit you have a choice. You can continue on the green path dropping back to the lakeside walk or continue on the path to your left, enjoying height for a little longer before gradually dipping to reach the wallside path used on the outward journey, opposite an isolated tree trunk in a field.

A left turn takes you back to the ladder stile and a retracing of steps to the car park.

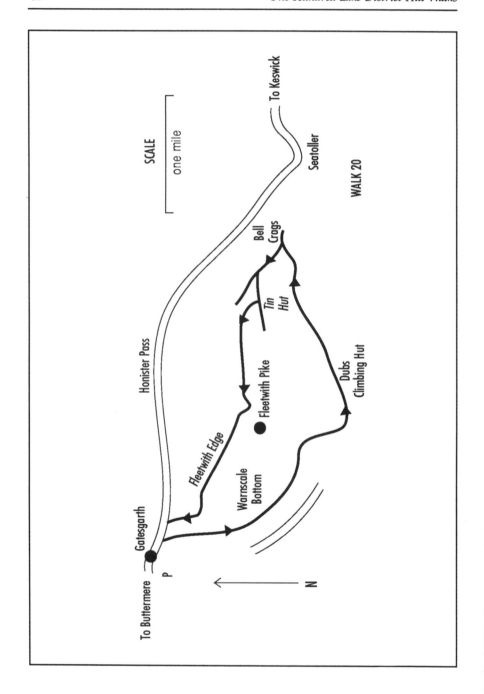

20. Fleetwith Pike and Warnscale Bottom

A moderate walk with glorious views, particularly of Buttermere, Crummock Water and Loweswater from the top of Fleetwith Pike (2106ft/648m).

Distance: 4ml/6.4km

Amount of climbing: 2106ft/648m

How to get there:

By car. Parking at Gatesgarth (MR195149).

Refreshments: Buttermere (MR186169).

Nearest tourist information: See Walk 1

Walk along Honister Pass towards Seatoller for about 100 yards and take the right-hand small wooden bridleway sign pointing straight on. After about 40 minutes easy going, arrive at Warnscale Bottom as the path veers left in front of an attractive waterfall, away from Warnscale Beck and a footbridge, which you do not cross.

The path winds upwards for a few hundred feet with Haystacks, Scarth Gap pass and High Crag across to the right. Keep going on where a path comes in from the right and after a bit more climbing reach Dubs Hut, originally a building for Dubs Quarry but later used by Keswick Mountain Club and now a place of refuge (complete with bunks) for fell wanderers caught in the dark.

Keep to the right of the hut as you travel on with Grey Knots to the right, Dale Head to the left and the Borrowdale Range of hills ahead. At cross-paths at Bell Crags, turn left. After a few yards, take a left fork. Opposite a tin hut, go right along a quarry track. On a bearing of 20 degrees with Great Gable behind in the distance pass a series of small tarns to the right and left. Soon you are rewarded for your efforts by gaining the summit of Fleetwith Pike, from which can be had a panoramic view of three lakes in one look – Buttermere, Crummock Water and Loweswater.

It is all downhill from here, down the tricky crags of Fleetwith Edge and then a piece of greenery. At a waymark, the path veers right by a safety fence, and winds past an erosion sign where a white cross can be seen up on a crag. A path goes up to the cross and there one may read a plinth that was erected by the friends of Fanny Mercer, accidentally killed in 1887, presumably at that spot. Down the grassy embankment to Honister Pass, turn left to return to the car park.

Buttermere from Fleetwith

21. Buttermere Fell

Buttermere is one of the best-known spots in the Lake District. Ask anyone, however, to identify Buttermere Fell and they may be hard pressed. Although marked on the OS map it is not as well known as nearby Red Pike, Whiteless, Robinson and Hindscarth. Buttermere Fell covers Warnscale and High Crag and is the "drop" to the southern shore of Buttermere on the last leg of this challenging trek.

Distance: 6.4ml/10km

Amount of climbing: 2600ft/800m

How to get there:

By car: National Trust car park (MR174172); rear of Fish Hotel (MR172168).

By bus: Mountain Goat (Keswick-Buttermere service).

Refreshments: Farm café, Fish and Bridge Hotels and Trevere Guest House (cups of tea only), all in Buttermere.

Nearest tourist information: See Walk 15

Follow the track to the left of the Bridge and Fish hotels. Through a wicket gate; then take the extreme of two right-hand turnings. A kissing gate at a "Buttermere National Trust" sign takes you on to a right turn over a footbridge with Buttermere lake to the left. Straight on through another kissing gate at the side of Sour Milk Gill waterfall and across another footbridge and ladder stile at the side of a gate. Take the high road. After a few yards our path goes right up rock-hewn steps. A climb of 100 feet or so takes us through a small gate to continue on the same terrain. Winding towards the summit of Red Pike, on the opposite approach to that in Walk 18, the way is grassy for a while before stone steps start again. Long before Pike top is reached, however, cairns lead to a tranquil tarn; an ideal spot for lunch. To the right of the tarn, known as Bleaberry, probably because there are plenty of bleaberries around here, continue up the shale path, reaching a variety of eroded ways and plenty of scree before the goal of the first peak on this walk is reached.

From the shelter of Red Pike, follow a southerly compass bearing with Ennerdale Water down to the right. There is a panoramic view of

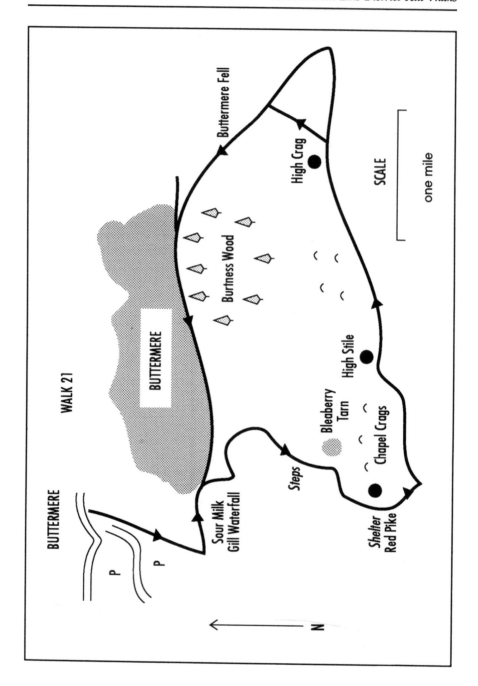

Bleaberry Tarn to the left before starting the 61 metre climb to the top of High Stile by the edge of Chapel Crags.

Off High Stile onto High Crag, there is a magnificent view of Buttermere and the valley down to the left. We are on·a ridge called Gamlin End. Just past a minute tarn, after dropping off High Crag take a left-hand path leading down to the Scarth Gap path.

A left turn (north) here and we are on our way towards Buttermere and the valley that looks so beckoning. It is a descent of some 585 metres, or 1,901 feet, but a wonderful walk. The path is easy to follow through a wall gap, over a waterfall, a footbridge over another waterfall and alongside a plantation, at the end of which is a split of tracks.

Of the two to the left, take the one towards the lake and turn left through Burtness Wood, where there is a seat for the weary. Through the delightful wood for nearly a mile, pass through a small gate and over a footbridge just after the Red Pike turn-off, taken on the outward trek. Now it is familiar ground as steps are retraced back to Buttermere. It is worth viewing the memorial to author Alfred Wainwright in Buttermere Church.

Buttermere Fells from Buttermere

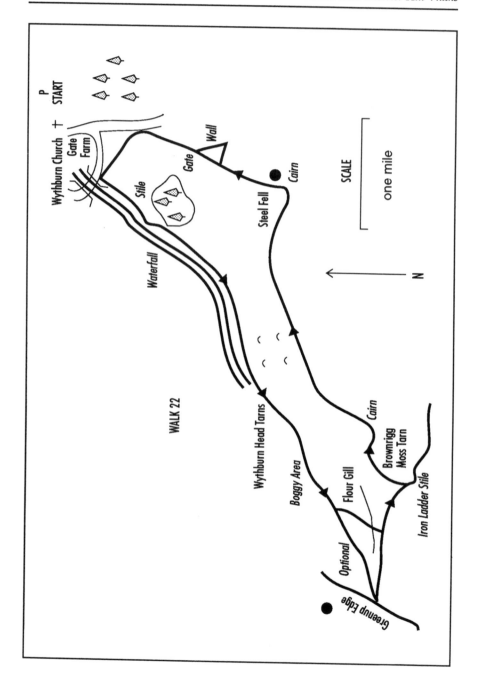

22. The Wythburn Fells

The panoramic view of Thirlmere from the top of Steel Fell is a sight to behold. It is the last high viewpoint on this delightful round, which can take in an optional climb to Greenup Edge.

Walking distance: 6.8ml/11km

Amount of climbing: 1040ft/320m (1527ft/470m optional)

How to get there:

By car: Steel End car park (MR320129).

By bus: Keswick-Lancaster service (CMS).

Refreshments: Thirlspot Inn (MR316177) and Grasmere.

Nearest tourist information: Red Bank Road, Grasmere. Telephone Grasmere (05394) 35245 and see Walk 1.

On the Grasmere side of Wythburn Church (MR324136) on the A591 road, take the Armboth road for a few hundred yards to a North West Water car park in trees on the right. Out of the car park, turn left. Immediately over the bridge spanning Wyth Burn go through a small right-hand gate.

Follow the burn now, over a fence stile and keeping a footbridge on the right, the way is rocky before passing a waterfall and Wythburn Head Tarns, from where the route, on a 240 degree bearing is extremely boggy. As the path peters out aim for Flour Gill on a 220 degree bearing and cross the Gill where it lines up parallel with Greenup Edge, the highest point immediately ahead. (This is the point where there is an optional route to the top of Greenup Edge). If you do this, you descend by the path reached by crossing the Gill,

Over the Gill, turn left along the path you will already be on if you have gone to the Edge summit. Aim for an iron ladder stile. Another left turn, at this isolated ladder stile, takes you alongside a broken old county boundary fence, on North 20 degrees. Brownrigg Moss Tarn is on the right and a few hundred yards along, there are another couple of tarns before the climb to the summit of Steel Fell (1797ft/553m).

Here are the sights to behold, not just of Thirlmere but of surrounding fells such as Helm Crag to the right of the approach to the summit cairn, and Helvelleyn at 45 degrees. Head north over a fence stile to start a dip of more than 1000 feet towards a wood. Pass through a gate in a wall and head for the wood. At the left-hand wall corner, just past the end of the wood, pass through a large National Park gate. Across a beck go to right-hand signs and through a right-hand gate on a bridleway sign. This takes you through West Head Farmyard. Reaching the lane, turn right and over the bridge you are on familiar ground on the return to the car park.

Looking towards the central fells and Greenup Edge

23. Glaramara

This is a walk that typifies Lakeland life in all its glory. Even the drive along the B5289 through the Borrowdale valley is a sight to behold. Both sides of the road are flanked by fells for several miles, not to mention Derwent Water, which provides a bonus for part of the route out of Keswick.

Distance: 8ml/12km

Amount of climbing: 2746ft/845m

How to get there:

By car. Parking on lane short of Seathwaite Farm (MR236121).

By bus: Keswick-Seatoller service (CMS), then walk along Seathwaite Lane (one mile).

Refreshments: Seathwaite Farm

Nearest tourist information: See Walk 1

The grandeur of the mountains is seen as you turn off the B5289 at Seatoller, along the mile-long lane to Seathwaite. Here is where the traditional country scene all starts. You may be fortunate, as were Bill (the photographer), his twin sister Yvonne and me, to see the farmer and his dogs guiding a flock of sheep into their pen. When one of the dogs took a nip at the farmer his language was as colourful as the scenery! That, however, is by the way. The way ahead forms a wonderful round taking in Grains Gill, Glaramara (2560ft/783m), gorgeous panoramic views and part of Harry Appleyard's long-distance Allerdale Ramble as an alternative return trek.

From where you have parked, walk on along the lane and through the farm yard. Continue along the side of Grains Gill and over a stile with Taylorgill Force to the right before reaching Stockley Bridge. This is a fine, packhorse bridge built in typical Cumbrian stone. Cross it and immediately turn left alongside a wall. There is a steady climb before a T-junction of tracks at the head of Grains Gill, the one to the right going to the popular Sprinkling Tarn. Your way is left. Soon it dips left across a ford (the second such crossing on the way here); continue (east) to rise over several crags.

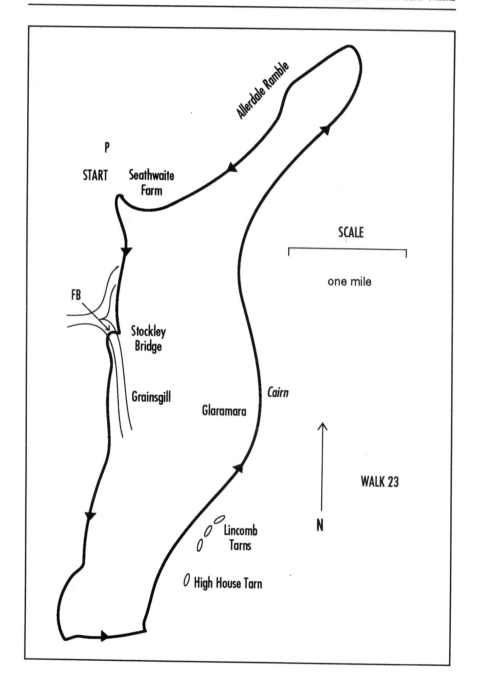

Taylorgill, on the trek to Glaramara

At cross-tracks near Esk Hause shelter go left over more crags and past a few tarns on the right before eventually getting to the chief summit of them all, Glaramara. There are magnificent views from this point and all the way up at various stages of Derwent Water, Great Gable, Great End, the Langdales and even Helvellyn and Blencathra. For us the adventure started on the downward trek from the shelter and cairn on the top of Glaramara. The crags are tricky and each step requires care.

Safely down we searched for a mapped path to the left which should lead down to Seathwaite. We spotted a line of cairns shooting off left and soon found a path only to discover that it looped back to the main path dropping to Combe Beck. I saw a green path in the direction of Seathwaite just before the main path dropped to the beck. I thought I would investigate its ability to give us a short cut to Seathwaite. By that time Bill and Yvonne had disappeared from sight. I did not know which way they had gone. It was a late September day with the night drawing in. So I decided to get off the tops and follow the main path down to Combe Gill. I suggest this is the most reliable route. It takes you to a farm lane near Seatoller. Turn left and where the farm lane goes to the farm keep straight on between walls and follow the footpath signs taking you along the Allerdale Ramble long-distance route to Seathwaite.

What about Bill and Yvonne? They had been waiting at the car for half an hour. They had used the safe route that I eventually followed and said they had shouted to me from behind a rock. Such things can happen on the fells. So take extra care on this one.

24. Dodd, Longside Edge and Ullock Pike

This is a walk with several permutations. There is a chance to visit a 17th century manor house, Mirehouse, associated with Francis Bacon; to have a stroll through a forest, scramble up the fell side and enjoy glorious views from Dodd, Ullock Pike and Longside Edge; even go to the top of Skiddaw if feeling energetic.

Walking distance: 5.8ml/8.4km

Amount of climbing: 3060ft/950m

How to get there:

By car: Dodd Wood car park (MR235281)

By bus: Keswick-Carlisle-Workington-Whitehaven (CMS). Keswick-Carlisle (CMS).

Refreshments: Sawmill café (at car park).

Nearest tourist information: See Walk 1

The safest way to reach Dodd summit (1612ft/502m) is to obtain a forest trail leaflet from the Sawmill café and follow the Long Walk, marker posted green. There would appear several permutations. Whatever you do, there is a maze of zig-zagging tracks to follow. From Dodd is a straight forward way taking in the slopes of Skiddaw, the inviting Longside Edge and Ullock Pike before dropping back to Mirehouse car park.

I recommend that with your back to the main road, embark on the track which starts to the right of the café front and pass a footbridge along an uphill right fork. Through attractive woodland with a gill down to the left, ignore a right-hand track before taking the next right.

Climbing again, turn left at a red and green marker post to reach a further such post and another left turn. Just before the brow of this track, at another red and green marker, go right.

At the crown of this path, branch right on a broad track to go left at the next green marker post. This bends left at a loop in the path, which is only an alternative, to emerge from the wood on a cone-strewn way. The

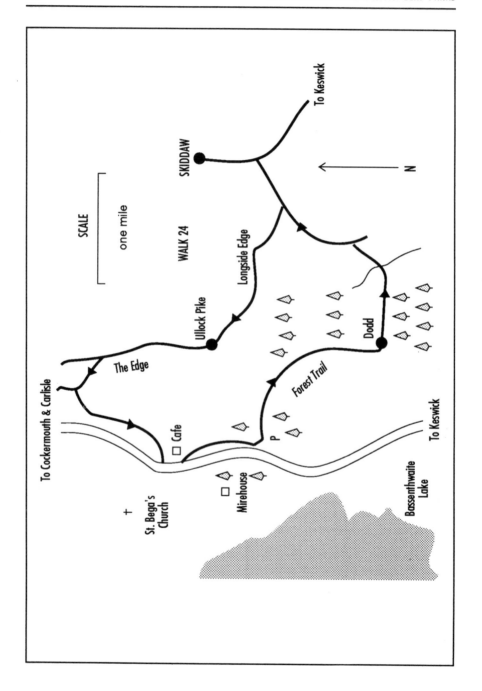

way is straight on where another path goes right in the direction of the distant Derwent Water.

This is a well trodden steep path which winds left to reach the sign saying 300 metres to Dodd summit, where there is a memorial to John Lole and Ian Sandelands, of the 1st Seaton Scout Group, 1980.

Then, retrace steps and continue along the bottom path zig-zagging to a broad track, which I crossed to surmount a stile and embark on an expedition up the slopes of Skiddaw.

Eventually, the well-worn route towards Skiddaw's mighty summit is reached. Go left for a few yards and with the awesome looking path towards Skiddaw to the right, go left again along the ridge of Longside Edge. Over one mound, Ullock Pike (2385ft/734m) is the next one. The path is undulating. Just before the final hump on the ridge, look down leftwards to a farm in the valley. A green path leads that way. Follow it and soon branch off left towards the woods. Go left at the fence, dropping on a scree surface through a couple of small gates, the second one with a stile at the side.

You emerge by the side of the Ravenstone Hotel close to the A591 Keswick-Carlisle road. Turn left under the trees on the track which tells you Dodd Wood car park is 1¼ miles. It runs parallel with the road. It is not long before you are guided to the main road. After a few yards on the metal, you can walk along another parallel path. This comes out near the track leading to the car park, where I found a notice saying "Danger, do not proceed!" It is not far, however, along the road to the car park and café entrance where it all started. Buses stop outside and the car park is to the right.

Mirehouse stately home is down a track off the Carlisle-bound side of the main road. The first bit of the house was built by the 8th Earl of Derby in 1666 as a lodge for his Cumbrian estates visits. There is an admission charge. St Bega's Norman Church in the grounds is a special feature.

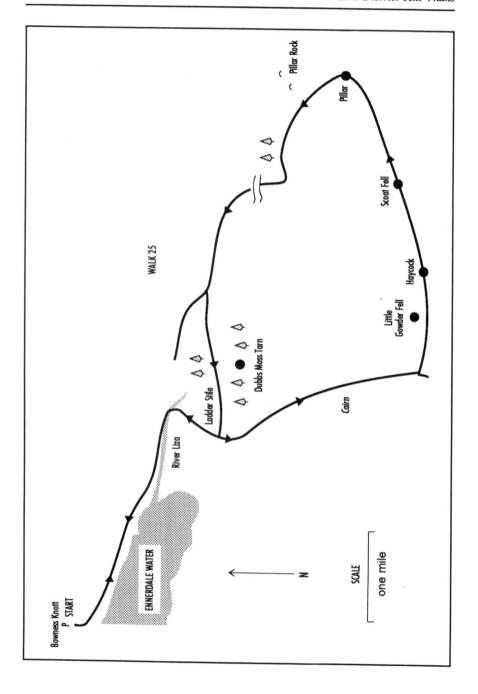

Pillar Rock

Pillar

Scoat Fell

Haycock

Little
Gowder Fell

Cairn

Dubbs Moss Tarn

WALK 25

Ladder Stile

River Liza

Bowness Knott
P START

ENNERDALE WATER

N

SCALE
one mile

25. Haycock, Scoat Fell and Pillar

A fox skipping its way across the skyline into Ennerdale Forest was a bonus for photographer Bill and myself as we neared the end of this challenging jaunt taking in three major peaks of the Ennerdale Horseshoe – and as always the views are glorious.

Walking distance: 11ml/16.5km

Amount of climbing: 2918ft/898m

How to get there:

By car. Bowness Knott car park (MR110154).

Refreshments: Ennerdale Bridge (MR070159), inns and shop.

Nearest tourist information: See Walk 2

From Bowness Knott, follow a 120 degrees south-east bearing along the Ennerdale Lakeside forestry road (with your back to the direction from which you entered the car park). As the lake ends after just over a mile and just under two kilometres of road walking, join the River Liza path.

Where it emerges at a broad track, cross the bridge and continue alongside Woundell Beck and Silvercove Beck. Cross a footbridge before leaving the forestry and start a steady climb on a rock-strewn path for 1³/₄ miles (2.5km) over a couple of cairns and Little Gowder Fell to Haycock (2598ft/979m) with cairns and shelter.

After a short stay at the first of our peaks, drop and climb again to Scoat Fell, which is in two "lumps" – Great Scoat Fell (2606ft/802m) and Little Scoat Fell (2839ft/841m). The third and final goal is Pillar (2928ft/892m) the eighth highest peak in the Lake District National Park. Looking north there is a splendid view of Pillar Rock, standing only a few feet or metres from Pillar itself and a classic rock climb. As you proceed on a 300 degrees north-west bearing there is an even better glimpse taking in the full width of the rock.

Continuing on this path, drop about 1,000 feet to Ennerdale Forest and take the second stile (the one near a small gate) leading on a path through the trees.

Walk now in the opposite direction of the Pillar signs and cross a broad track into more trees. This path passes on the left Moss Dubbs Tarn and carries on to take you out of the forestry via a ladder stile onto a familiar broad track ahead and over the bridge we used over the River Liza on the outward journey.

Use the river path again or if you think you can go faster on the metal surface use the forestry road for the $1^3/_4$m/2.5km bash back to the car park.

Ennerdale is the ideal valley from which to view Pillar, in the centre of this picture, taken from Moss Dubbs

The South West

This is covered by the South West sheet of the English Lakes Outdoor Leisure Ordnance Survey map.

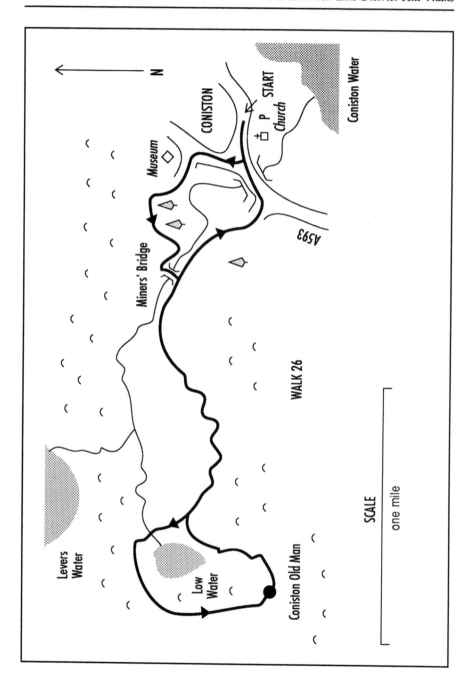

N

Coniston Water

START

P

Church

CONISTON

Museum

A593

Miners' Bridge

WALK 26

SCALE

one mile

Levers
Water

Low
Water

Coniston Old Man

26. Coniston Old Man

Coniston Old Man, to give it its affectionate title, but marked on maps as The Old Man of Coniston, towers above the village of the same name and its famous Water, graveyard of Donald Campbell and his Bluebird speed boat which sunk in pieces with him while he was attempting a world water speed record, in 1967.

Walking distance: 4.5ml/7.2km

Amount of climbing: 2317ft/713m

How to get there:

By car. Park behind Parish Church (MR302975).

By bus: See CMS timetable.

Refreshments: Coniston

Nearest tourist information: 16, Yewdale Road, Coniston. Telephone (0539) 441533

Walk to the centre of the village and go right, along the main street. On the near side of the museum is your track. At a junction of ways, go left. Keep Church Beck on your left, before crossing it at Miners Bridge, so called because of the former copper mines in the locality.

Your track continues by disused quarries to reach Low Water. Follow the right-hand bank and climb to a point where Levers Water is overlooked. Here start to turn round on a southerly bearing aiming for Coniston Old Man summit (2633ft/803m) cairn. Reaching a point where Coniston Water is visible in the distance, take an easterly bearing.

Scramble down back to Miners Bridge. Keep on the right of Church Beck. Continue along this path to reach Coniston beyond a pub, on the Torver road.

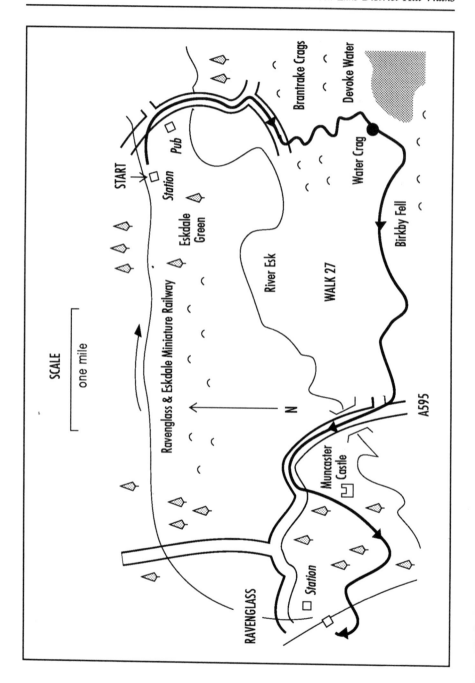

27. Brantrake and Water Crags, Devoke Water and Birkby Fell

This moderate jaunt taking in the remote Devoke Water, starts with a ride on a miniature railway.

Walking distance: 8ml/12.6km

Amount of climbing: 990ft/300m

How to get there:

By car: Parking is in Ravenglass village near the main line railway station (split from "Ratty" station by a footbridge) MR085964

By train: Cumbria Coast Line to and from Ravenglass.

Refreshments: Ravenglass and Muncaster Castle.

Nearest tourist information: Ravenglass and Eskdale Railway. Telephone (0229) 717278.

From the car park, cross the footbridge to join the "Ratty" – the nickname for the Ravenglass and Eskdale Miniature Railway.

Book a single ticket to The Green, which you leave near the road bridge. Turn right over the River Esk. Take the first lane to the right just before "sheep" sign. Just before a right-hand car parking space, use a step stile in left-hand trees. Go left alongside a stone wall. Start to climb behind the farm. Contour left on a broad green path onto Brantrake Crags (849ft/259m). The path keeps to the left of boulders before levelling out. Continue on a south-east bearing. With the rocky Water Crag (1000ft/305m) to the right, cross a tributary of Linbeck Gill and continue for 1.6ml/1km.

Following the same direction and keeping clear of a plantation to the right, arrive at Devoke Water. Maintain direction to the far nearside corner (spot the pump house at the lake top) and turn right on a broad track over Birkby Fell (840ft/256m).

Fork right almost level with the start of woodland a short distance to the left. Head for the Irish Sea and reach the A595 road. Right, over the River Esk (Muncaster) bridge and climb round the left-hand bend. Go through a left-hand gate at "footpath to church" sign. Out of the churchyard, turn left through Muncaster Castle grounds.

At a T-junction of drives, go right, and then left on a path across a lawn into woods. At the end, cross a stile onto open fell. Go diagonally left over a hillock. Just short of more woods turn right to cross a stile onto a path through trees.

Go right at a drive, then right again at a T-junction. Just short of the village road take a left-hand path at the side of a small building back to the car park.

To shorten the walk, you could, but it is not recommended because of unpredictable tides, take the Waberthwaite path at Muncaster Bridge and cross the River Esk ford near Waberthwaite Church. Then skirt castle grounds and walk along the shore to Ravenglass, clipping 1ml/1.6km off the walk.

The pump house on the banks of Devoke Water overlooked by Brantrake Crags and Water Crag

28. Stainton Fell

An extremely remote fell walk in country rarely explored by the average rambler.

Walking distance: 5.1ml/8.2km

Amount of climbing: 1111ft/342m

How to get there:

By car. Verge parking is available on the A595 road near Devoke Water footpath sign at Dyke, MR112951.

Refreshments: Muncaster Castle.

Nearest tourist information: See Walk 27

Walk along the main road in a southerly direction for about a third of a mile (less than a kilometre) to Broad Oak, with a telephone box on the right and a large farm complex on the left.

Cross the farm cattle grid to just short of Stainton Farm, MR126947. Cross a footbridge onto open Stainton Fell. Keep Stainton beck below left as you cross the fence via a stile and continue over a ladder stile.

Diagonally left takes you towards The Knott (1086ft/331m) between the beck and a plantation. Through two successive gates, the rightwards track bends in a half-moon to pass through another gate on the same line as the last one.

Over boggy ground, cross a fence between The Knott and White Pike (1450ft/442m, cairn) and go through the gap between the two peaks on a north-north-west bearing. A view of Ravenglass Estuary to the left, follow the sheep trod right (north-north-east).

Make for the right of the white house in the distance. Down crags, keep north. Through a gap of small rocks, change course to east along a rising grassy track. After a few yards head for the Irish Sea. There is a dome on the left-hand hill as the sea and main road draw closer.

Muncaster Bridge can be seen spanning the River Esk. It is a tidy drop over sometimes precarious rocks to road level. Find a track going diagonally left down the hillside to a sunken lane leading to the main road opposite Graymains Farm. Left for about a kilometre will return you to your car.

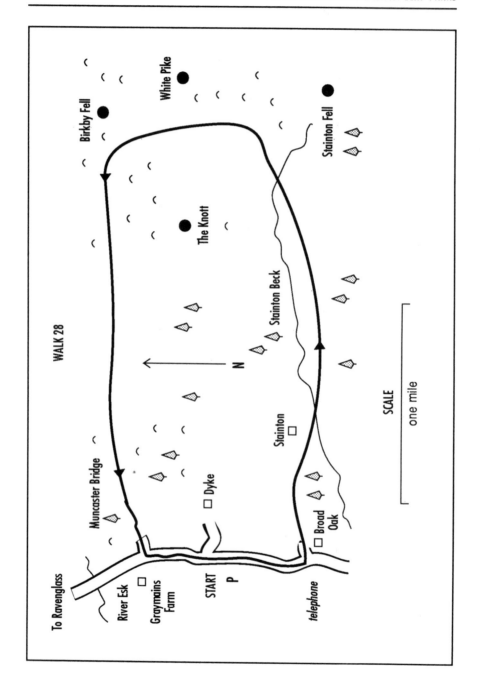

29. Irton Pike and Mitredale Forest

This walk takes in Irton Pike and Mitredale Forest, one of the most attractive areas of woodland in Western Lakeland.

Walking distance: 5ml/8km

Amount of climbing: 656ft/200m

How to get there:

By car. Parking is available at the old quarry on the Santon Bridge-Eskdale road, marked Pit (dis) on the map, (MR121012).

Refreshments: Santon Bridge Hotel (MR109017).

Nearest tourist information: Craft Shop, Gosforth (MR069037). Telephone (0946) 725287

From the car, go back along the road for a few yards to surmount a stile at the side of a gate. Rise by the side of the wood to reach open fell and enjoy splendid views of Wast Water.

Irton Pike (656ft/200m) is the unmistakable summit to the left. You can climb it if you wish. Returning from the peak, follow a fell path running alongside Mitredale Forest, entered at a stone wall gap stile after keeping an east bearing.

In the forest, cross over the first broad track you reach, downhill through the trees to cross a second forestry road. Your path goes slightly diagonally right to cross two more forestry roads.

Round a right-hand bend, your path goes through the rhododendrons and bends left and right over rough rocks. Over a beck stone, a path and fire sign come in from the left. Soon you arrive at a lovely old packhorse bridge, a typical scene throughout Cumbria, whether inside or outside the National Park. After admiring the babbling beck below, about turn – following the path running parallel with the beck.

A climb brings you to a cross-paths junction, where the way is left, again flanked by rhododendrons. The compass bearing is west and the ground is a combination of wet and rocks as the path wends between a stone

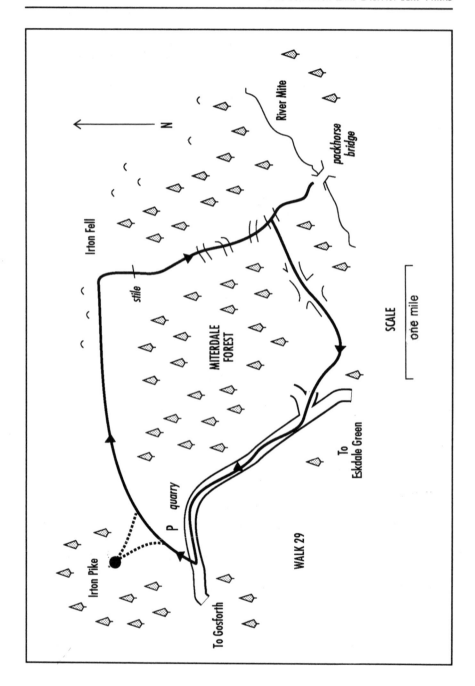

wall and bushes. At the next forestry road, go left again and through a stile at the side of a red iron gate to run left to the main road.

A right turn here gives you half-a-mile's pleasant walking along a country road that is not all that busy, back to the old quarry car park.

The view from Irton Fell towards Wasdale

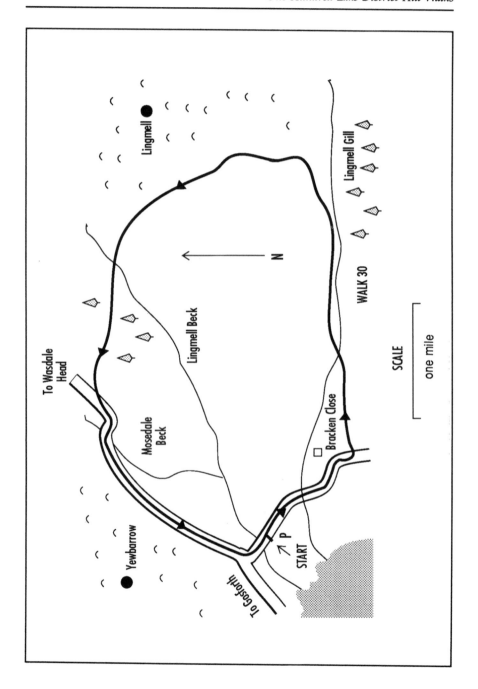

30. Wasdale

A lowland walk at the foot of some of the finest mountain scenery in Europe, such as the Scafells and Great Gable.

Walking distance: 2.5ml/4km

Amount of climbing: 857ft/265m

How to get there:

By car. Park courtesy of the National Trust near Brackenclose camp site, Wasdale. (MR182074).

Refreshments: Wasdale Head Hotel and farms.

Nearest tourist information: Barn Door Shop, Wasdale Head. Telephone (0946) 726384.

Return to the side road from the far end of the car park. Follow the track over the bridge to a way-marker. Go left towards the Fell and Rock Climbing Club building. Pass through a small gate in the left-hand corner of the croft.

Now start a climb of about 1000ft/300m above sea level to a point where the fellside flattens briefly before the next stage of the ascent towards Lingmell (2649ft/807m).

At the short, flat bit, the highest point of the walk, with views of the whole expanse of Wast Water and the mighty Screes, rising majestically to more then 2000ft/609m and sweeping down alarmingly to the left-hand edge of the lake, take the path going left. It is the first left from the bottom.

Over this rock-strewn way on this part of the Scafell Massif, Lingmell Beck soon comes into view. In about 1.2ml/9.3km from the turn, the path crosses the beck by a footbridge.

Wasdale Head Hotel and scattered farmsteads have already been spotted as low level is reached again. Grass and bush have now taken over from rocks and a double bridleway and a footpath sign is reached at gates and step stiles.

Your way, however, is along the road for about 1ml/1.6km, crossing the attractive pack horse bridge over Mosedale Beck and keeping company with the babbling beck down on the left before arriving at the Wasdale Head Hall Farm and camp site sign where you entered to get to the car park, and, where after surmounting another bridge, this time over Lingmell Beck, you return.

Over Wastwater to Yewbarrow, Great Gable and Lingmell

31. Muncaster Fell

Another chance to visit the 13th century Muncaster Castle, grounds and amenities, coupled with a breezy climb over Muncaster Fell and finishing with a bracing stroll along Ravenglass seashore.

Walking distance: 9.5ml/15km

Amount of climbing: 750ft/231m

How to get there:

By car. Park as for Walk 27

By train: See Walk 27

Refreshments: See Walk 27

Nearest tourist information: See Walk 27

This time there is no ride on "La'al Ratty". Use cross-country paths to reach the A595 road at a point between the War Memorial and Home Farm (MR093966). A right turn takes you past Muncaster Castle entrance in 0.2ml/0.3km to a right-hand bend and double bridleway signs. Take the one to Eskdale and Hardknott. Take this over Muncaster Fell (750ft/231m) to reach a T-junction of tracks. Go right over the step-stile on the sign for Muncaster Head.

Drop to a further step-stile and at the next T-junction of tracks, near Muncaster Head Farm, go right on the Muncaster sign at a gate and stile, and then through another gate or over another stile alongside. Take the bridleway signed at the sunken gate and make across the golf course for the left-hand woods, which you keep to the left before passing through a small gate and later over a stile at the side of a large gate.

The path can get churned before you emerge at a gate and stile and T-junction of tracks. Right here to cross a private drive to the main road. A right turn goes uphill for a left-hand turn signed Muncaster Church. At a drive-way which is also a public footpath through the castle grounds, turn left. Use the map to reach the shore. Go right and reach Main Street, Ravenglass, with life-belt and notices on a wall. Up the street, see the Pennington Arms and Post Office and a signed right-hand footpath for the railway station.

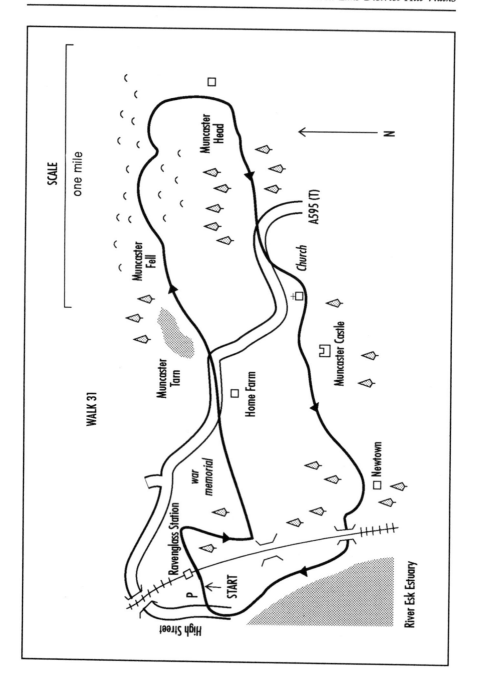

32. Ponsonby Fell

Ponsonby Fell (1020ft/310m) is ideally suited for dull overcast days when the surrounding fells are in mist leaving the lower heights for exploration.

Walking distance: 10ml/16km

Amount of climbing: 860ft/260m

How to get there:

By car. Main village car park in Gosforth (MR068036)

By bus: Whitehaven-Seascale service

Refreshments: Gosforth

Nearest tourist information: See Walk 29

Take the village street to the east forking left onto the Wasdale road after a short distance. After a further 3.4 mile where the road turns sharply right to cross the River Bleng, continue ahead on what becomes a tarmaced forestry track on the western bank of the Bleng.

At Blengdale Lodge, the track crosses the river and becomes a muddy track that divides in two. Take the lower riverside path for 3.4 miles, where the track again divides. Cross the footbridge and return to the ford continuing steeply uphill on the forestry track to reach the main forestry road heading north-north-east out of the forest towards Scalderskew.

After half a mile, a footpath sign to Scargreen is reached. Follow this through gate and ascent to the summit of Ponsonby Fell.

From the summit aim for a gate on the Scargreen path to the west (260 degrees). Go through gate and follow field edge crossing the fence after 300 yards to arrive at an enclosed track above Laverock How. Follow the track to Scargreen.

At Scargreen ford turn left past farm buildings and after 150 yards go ahead through gate by wooden footpath sign onto a wide muddy track. Continue along the track to arrive on a farm road south of Hurlbarrow. (Use stile just before farm road to cross hedge).

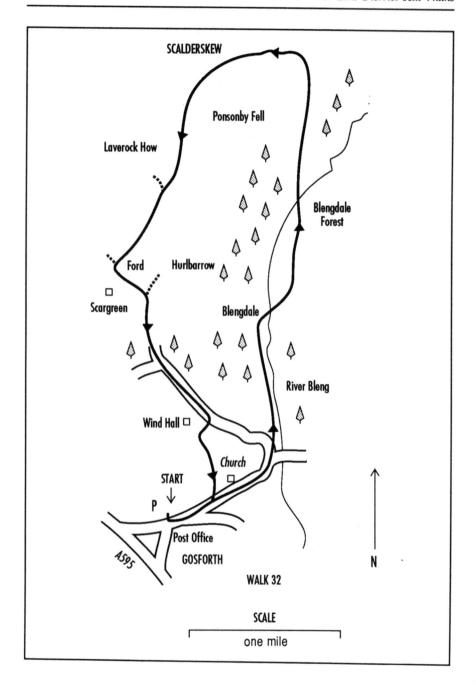

SCALDERSKEW

Ponsonby Fell

Laverock How

Blengdale
Forest

Ford   Hurlbarrow

Scargreen

Blengdale

River Bleng

Wind Hall

Church

START

P

Post Office

A595

GOSFORTH

WALK 32

N

SCALE

one mile

Turn right on track and follow it for three-quarters of a mile to minor road. Here turn left to Wind Hall farm where signposted footpath heads right onto enclosed track. At the second stile, turn left to the brow of the hill and descend to Gosforth to arrive at the church. Turn right on the road for the car park.

Ponsonby Fell from Blengdale

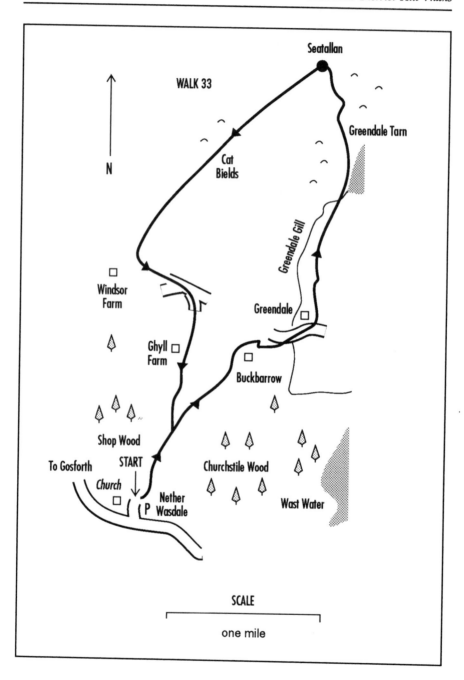

33. Greendale Tarn and Seatallan

A scenic route combining a distinct but rarely visited summit, a small tarn and a pleasant climb alongside a steep mountain beck.

Walking distance: 9ml/14.3km

Amount of climbing: 2180ft/670m

How to get there:

By car: Ample parking is to be found outside the church at Nether Wasdale, MR125041.

Refreshments: Pubs in Nether Wasdale

Nearest tourist information: See Walk 29

From church take the footpath sign along the track, through two gates to arrive at Church Stile campsite. Here follow track right to head through clearing between Churchstile and Shop woods, (keep close to Shop Wood), to arrive at a stile in the wall. Cross this and continue to reach gate. Go through gate and after 70 yards turn right over a derelict wall to reach a further wall and signpost. Follow "Buckbarrow" sign over field to reach a wall stile on the left of a gate. Go over this and at the end of the second field head through a gate on left to reach a farm track to Buckbarrow and the Wasdale road. Here turn right to Greendale.

Past Greendale turn left on a clear signposted track that leads up the eastern side of Greendale Gill to reach Greendale Tarn. At the tarn continue on the western edge to head uphill left at a suitable point to reach the summit of Seatallan (2266ft/692m).

From the summit follow ridge south-east to a distant cairn at Cat Bields. From here continue ahead to reach bracken covered slopes above Windsor Farm through which a farm track is reached leading down to the road.

At the road turn left and after 100 yards turn right down the track to Ghyll Farm (Gill on OS map). Follow the track through a farm to where it forks. Here take the right fork which soon rejoins our outward bound route leading back to Nether Wasdale.

Walking towards Whin Rigg summit

34. Illgill Head

This is a fine walk with excellent views of Wasdale and Wastwater Screes.

Walking distance: 13ml/21km

Amount of climbing: 2247ft/685m

How to get there:

By car. Outside Nether Wasdale Church, a gravel area allows parking (MR125041).

Refreshments: See Walk 58

Nearest tourist information: See Walk 54

From the church head towards the distant Wastwater Screes and at the first road junction go right over the River Irt. After 70 yards go left on the bridleway signposted "Eskdale". Head straight over first field to reach a stile by a gate and continue to reach another stile on the edge of woodland. Here, carry on keeping the wall on your left, rising uphill to reach the brow; from here, wall and path start heading to the left and after 100 yards a small bridleway sign on the right is reached. Go along here to emerge at gate on open fell land from which an easy climb leads to the summit ridge.

The clear grassy summit ridge is followed up over Whin Rigg to reach the higher Illgill Head (1996ft/609m) with spectacular views of the precipitous Wastwater Screes on route.

From the summit continue downhill to reach the popular Wasdale – Eskdale crossing track. Turn left and continue downhill to arrive at Lingmell Gill, MR183074. By bridge turn left on the footpath signposted "Lakeshore" to reach Wasdale Hall farm. As track swings left into farm go straight on over a stile on a clear path that runs to the end of the lake.

The path alongside the lake requires care in places but arrives at a vehicle access track for the pumping station at its far end. Here follow the track through Easthwaite to reach a road junction where the path retraces your steps back to Nether Wasdale.

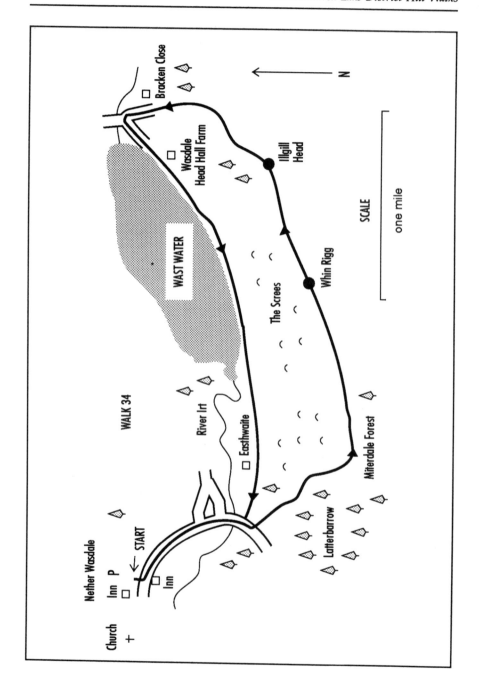

35. Caw Fell

Caw Fell commands an excellent view of southern Lakeland and, on a clear day, Morecambe Bay and Ingleborough can easily be seen.

Walking distance: 8ml/12.8km

Amount of climbing: 1770ft/540m

How to get there:

By car: Ample parking can be found on the grass verges south of the Ulpha bridge cattle grid, MR197930.

Refreshments: Ulpha Post Office (ice cream, crisps, drinks etc).

Nearest tourist information: Millom Folk Museum, St Georges Road, Millom. Telephone (0229) 772555.

From the cattle grid, walk south along the road to a bridleway sign on your left that leads to an isolated house called "Birks". At the house, do not go through a gate into wood but look for the path on the fellside that rises steeply through bracken parallel to Birks Wood boundary wall. Once the gradient eases, the indistinct path heads half right away from wood towards Hollow Moss Beck. Cross beck and contour round Stickle Pike to arrive near the summit on the Seathwaite to Broughton Mills road.

100 years below road summit on the Seathwaite side, a wide muddy track heads in a westerly direction. This track, Park Head Road, is followed for three-quarters of a mile to the foot of Caw Fell where a track is seen coming in on the right from Long Mire. Follow this track south-east and at its brow start scrambling to the summit of Caw Fell (1735ft/529m).

From the summit, return along Park Head Road to the fell road and descend towards Seathwaite to reach cattle grid, MR212935. Here find a small footpath sign on left that descends bracken-covered slopes to a wall stile in the bottom left-hand corner of a field. From stile turn left on track through two gates and at third gate by Birks Wood go through and turn right after 30 yards on unmarked footpath to reach gate into field. Continue in the same direction by the Duddon to reach Ulpha bridge.

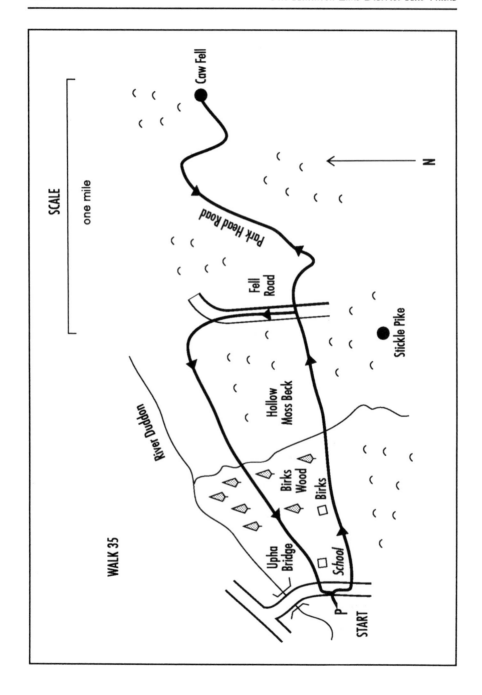

WALK 35

Looking north east from the Corney Fell road

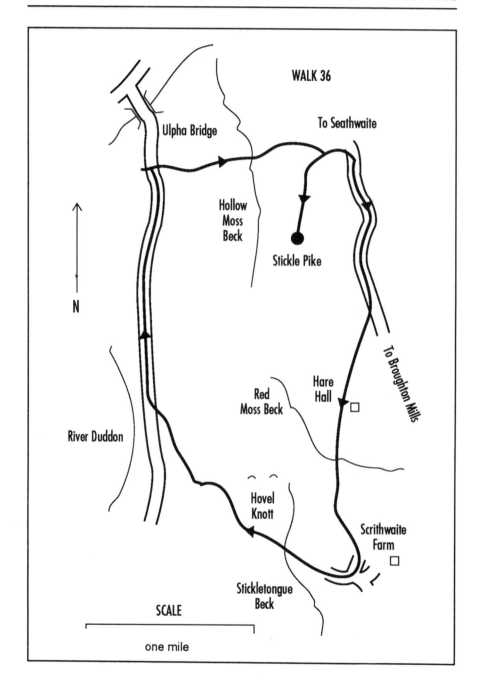

WALK 36

Ulpha Bridge

To Seathwaite

Hollow
Moss
Beck

Stickle Pike

N

Hare
Hall

Red
Moss Beck

To Broughton Mills

River Duddon

Hovel
Knott

Scrithwaite
Farm

Stickletongue
Beck

SCALE

one mile

36. Stickle Pike

This walk combines a prominent local fell together with a pleasant stroll round the Dunnerdale Fells.

Walking distance: 8ml/12.8km

Amount of climbing: 1480ft/450m

How to get there:

By car. Park as for Walk 35

Refreshments: See Walk 35

Nearest tourist information: See Walk 35

Start from the Ulpha Bridge cattle grid, MR197930 and follow the route as given for the Caw Fell walk as far as Hollow Moss Beck. From the beck do not be tempted to climb Stickle Pike from this direction but contour round to the north side where a clear path leads to the distinctly shaped summit (1231ft/375m).

Descend from the summit back to the Seathwaite – Broughton Mills road down the same track to arrive at the road summit. Here turn right and head downhill towards Hoses. At gate across the road, take the footpath on the right climbing steeply uphill with a wall on your left. As the wall turns left downhill, follow the wall past Hare Hall to arrive at Red Moss Beck. Cross the beck and after 30yds turn left through a rusted metal gate onto a track between walls. Continue on the track to arrive at a crossing track by Scrithwaite Farm.

From the crossing track, take the path to the west which rises round The Nursery on walled track and crosses Stickletongue Beck. Continue on the same path round the barn on your left and ascend past Hovel Knott. At the summit of the path, take the left fork and start to descend. After 150yds, the path again divides. Here go right and descend to the road below, arriving on the road by the side of the Duddon. Turn right and follow the road to Ulpha bridge.

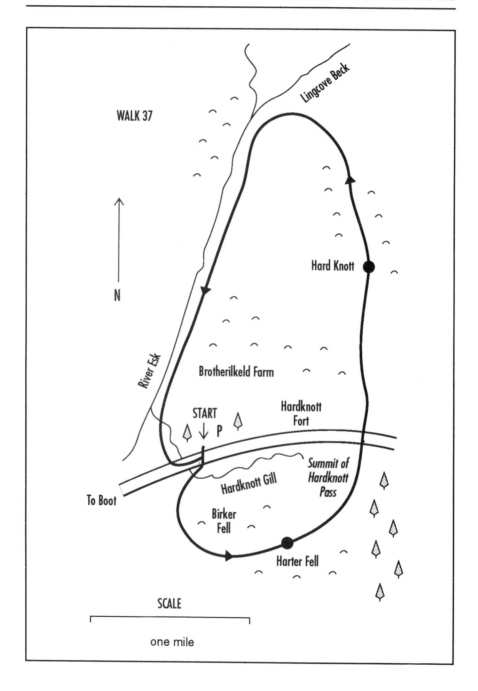

WALK 37

Lingcove Beck

N

River Esk

Hard Knott

Brotherilkeld Farm

START
P

Hardknott
Fort

To Boot

Hardknott Gill

Summit of
Hardknott
Pass

Birker
Fell

Harter Fell

SCALE

one mile

37. Harter Fell and Hard Knott

A walk encompassing two distinct summits, a mountain pass and a scenic walk along the River Esk.

Walking distance: 9.7ml/15.4km

Amount of climbing: 2760ft/840m

How to get there:

By car. Parking is to be found a few yards uphill of the cattle grid on the Hardknott Pass road, MR213011.

By train: Cumbria Coast Line to and from Ravenglass. Ravenglass and Eskdale Railway to and from Dalegarth. Proceed east to Hardknott Pass.

Refreshments: Eskdale and Boot.

Nearest tourist information: See Walks 27 and 29

From cattle grid, take the footpath signposted "Eskdale and Muncaster" over a stone bridge and through a gate to follow the clear path rising uphill in south-west direction. Follow the path until it reaches a wall and soon after take the unmarked path on left, (MR207002), that rises towards the summit of Harter Fell (2140ft/653m). (Note. If this path is missed, follow the main path until the edge of woodland and take the footpath on left to reach the summit).

The summit consists of several rocky outcrops giving good panoramic views. Our route follows the path through the summit outcrops to swing left after 50yds to head downhill towards the Hardknott – Wrynose Pass road on a clear easily followed path that eventually arrives at the road summit on the Hardknott Pass road. Here the route may be shortened by turning left down the road back to the car past Hardknott Fort, a prominent Roman fortification that is worth visiting either on the walk or at its end.

For those heading on, a steep climb over pathless terrain up the east edge of Border End is the reward to arrive at a plateau with Hard Knott summit (1803ft/549m).

From Hard Knott continue north along descending ridge aiming to arrive on a footpath at the junction of Lingcove Beck and River Esk. Here follow the clear path along the Esk keeping to the river's edge past Brotherlikeld Farm to arrive at the road. Turn left to reach your car.

Hardknott Fort and Hard Knott Fell

38. The Langdale Pikes

A scenic walk on easy clear paths with the summits of Harrison Stickle (2403ft/736m), Pike O'Stickle (2323ft/709m) and Loft Crag (2270ft/680m), all ascended.

Walking distance: 6.5ml/10.4km

Amount of climbing: 2,450ft/747m

How to get there:

By car. Parking is to be found in the NT car park at the Sticklebarn and New Dungeon Ghyll complex, MR295064.

Refreshments: New Dungeon Ghyll.

Nearest tourist information: Old Courthouse, Church Street, Ambleside. Telephone (05394) 32582.

From the car park, follow the path past the side of the toilets and behind the Sticklebarn to reach a stone stairway path running alongside Stickle Ghyll. Due to erosion, a wooden footbridge has been placed a short way up and the path follows the east edge of the ghyll to Stickle Tarn. At the tarn, stop and admire the rock face on the far side – "Pavey Ark". The usual route is to follow the tarn to the right to head up a clear path by Bright Beck but for those competent on rock and have no fear of heights, a good scramble up Jack's Rake can be contemplated. This is reached from the tarn by the scree path leading up to the steeply climbing edge (MR287078). There are no route-finding problems but there are only two exits, one at the top and one at the bottom. You climb at your own risk!

Whichever route you have chosen, you soon arrive at the grassy plateau by Thunacar Knott. Here, sit down and work out a route between the three close-lying summits. The suggested route is Harrison Stickle, Pike O'Stickle and then Loft Crag, as it is from the latter that the clear path heads downhill below Thorn Crag.

All the summits are easily reached and very popular being some of the most frequently climbed fells in the Lake District. The descent via Mark Gate is, however, not as popular as the ascent, but even here work has been carried out to prevent erosion. Such work does provide for easy route-finding and the car park is soon reached.

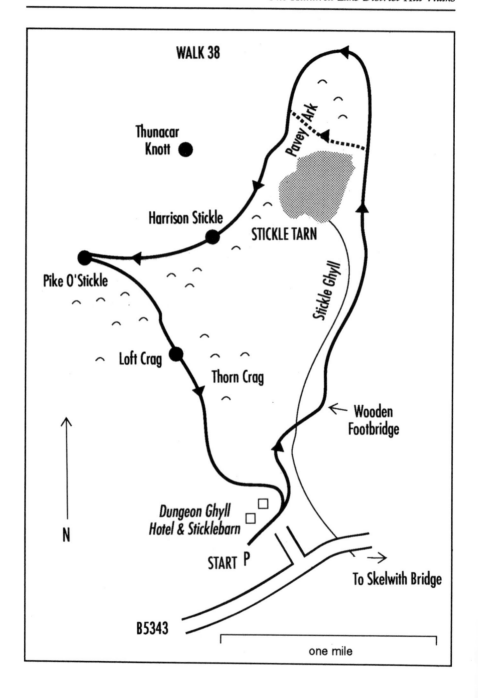

WALK 38

Thunacar
Knott ●

Pavey Ark

Harrison Stickle ●

STICKLE TARN

Pike O'Stickle ●

Stickle Ghyll

Loft Crag ●

Thorn Crag

← Wooden
Footbridge

N

Dungeon Ghyll
Hotel & Sticklebarn □
□

START P

To Skelwith Bridge →

B5343

one mile

39. Devoke Water and Rough Crag

The route around Devoke Water is a short easy route with a minimum of climbing involved.

Walking distance: 5ml/8km

Amount of climbing: 650ft/200m

How to get there:

By car. Parking is to be found at the crossroads near the summit of the Eskdale Green – Ulpha road (MR171977), where wide grassy verges allow off road parking.

By train: Ravenglass and Eskdale Miniature Railway to Eskdale Green, then additional walking of two miles each way between station and starting point.

Refreshments: Eskdale.

Nearest tourist information: See Walks 27 and 29.

From the crossroads take the wide stony track rising slightly uphill towards the tarn. At the track's summit Devoke Water comes into view and by careful searching a small track on the right can be seen crossing rough ground to reach Rough Crag. (It is possible to navigate round the tarn edge if an easier walk is required).

From the summit (1046ft/319m), the path drops gently down before rising to Water Crag from which an easy descent to the bridleway at the west edge of the tarn can be made.

Once on the bridleway turn left heading back along lakeside almost reaching the boathouse. Here, on crossing Hall Beck, look for a faint track on the east side of the beck that initially runs along the edge of the beck but continues ahead when the beck runs to the right. This faint track soon becomes a clear grassy track heading towards a distant copse and farm buildings at Woodend.

On arriving at Woodend, the path heads through a rusted iron gate to enter the farmyard and soon leads onto a tarmaced track which leads out over Woodend Pool onto the Ulpha road. Here turn left following the road back to the car keeping the magnificent views of Eskdale on your right.

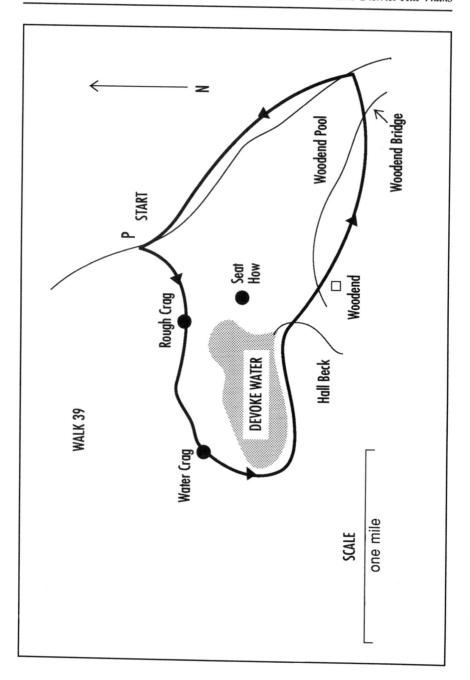

Rough Crag, Devoke Water

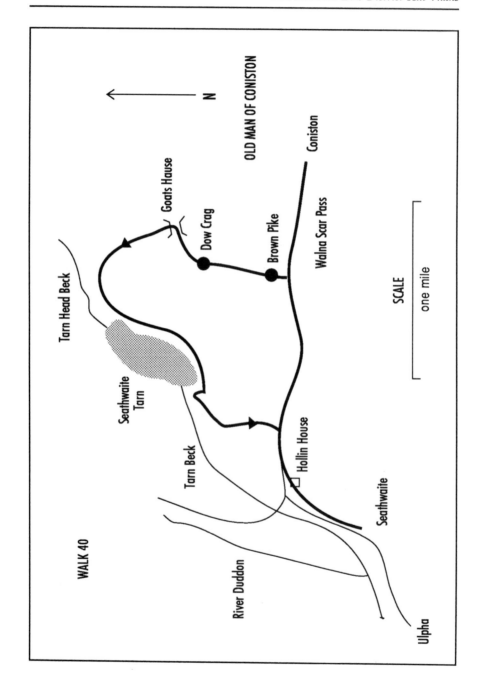

WALK 40

N

OLD MAN OF CONISTON

Goats House

Dow Crag

Brown Pike

Walna Scar Pass

Coniston

Tarn Head Beck

Seathwaite
Tarn

Tarn Beck

Hollin House

Seathwaite

River Duddon

Ulpha

SCALE

one mile

40. Seathwaite Tarn and Dow Crag

Dow Crag (2555ft/778m) provides for a good climb on mainly clear paths with no navigational difficulties. It also provides excellent views of the Old Man of Coniston, the Duddon valley and the Cumbrian and Lancastrian coastlines.

Walking distance: 8.5ml/13.6km

Amount of climbing: 2300ft/700m

How to get there:

By car. The start is at Seathwaite village where a small amount of parking may be found (MR228960).

Refreshments: Public house, Seathwaite.

Nearest tourist information: The Folk Museum, St Georges Road, Millom. Telephone Millom (0229) 772555.

From the village head north for half a mile to where the road starts to descend to cross Tarn Beck. Here fork right to Hollin House and keep to right at the next junction to arrive at open fellside at the start of the Walna Scar Road.

The track up Walna Scar is wide, clear and unmistakeable and crosses between the Duddon valley and Coniston. The track is followed to the Pass summit, where a short scramble to the left leads up Brown Pike and follows a clear ridge path to the summit of Dow Crag.

From the summit, the path descends to Goat's Hause (Hawse on the map), which lies at the head of the valley and is the lowest point between Dow Crag and Coniston Old Man. Here follow an indistinct path downhill towards Seathwaite Tarn. Before reaching Tarn Head Beck, head along the path on the left that leads along the south bank of the tarn, weaving in and out of the numerous boulders.

The path along the tarn soon arrives at the small dam at the head of a stony service track that serves the tarn reservoir. Here follow the track initially in a west-south-west direction as it gradually descends for some 1.5 miles, eventually arriving back at the foot of the Walna Scar Road from where we started our climb.

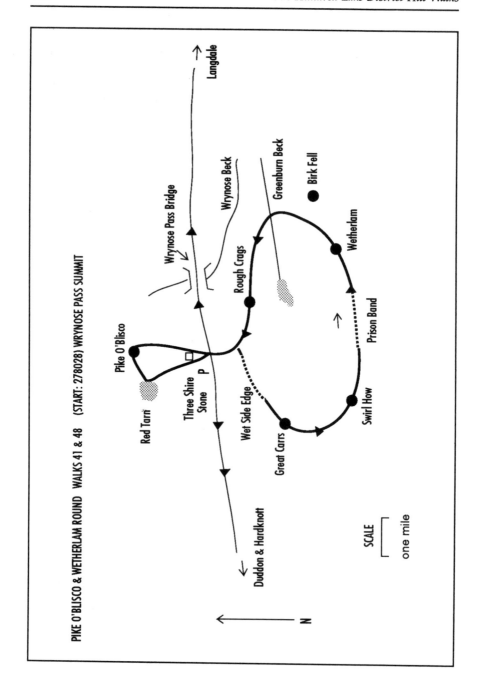

PIKE O'BLISCO & WETHERLAM ROUND   WALKS 41 & 48   (START: 278028) WRYNOSE PASS SUMMIT

41. The Wetherlam Round

The Wetherlam round is a hard but scenic circular route encompassing three ridge summits as it encircles Greenburn.

Walking distance: 7.2ml/11/5km

Amount of climbing: 3050ft/930m

How to get there:

By car. Parking space can be found off-road at the summit of Wrynose Pass (MR278028).

Refreshments: Boot.

Nearest tourist information: Boot Mill.

The start of this walk is at the summit of Wrynose pass, which allows for a shorter walk to the summit with a considerable reduction in the amount of climbing necessary. An alternative start from Little Langdale could be made, but this would have the effect of a long continual ascent at the beginning of the walk rather than the two less-demanding ascents in the route described here.

From the road summit, follow the clear unmarked path uphill towards Wet Side Edge. After a quarter of a mile, the gradient eases and approaches the Edge where spectacular views of Greenburn start to unfold. The route is straight forward round the valley head climbing Great Carrs (2575ft/780m), Swirl How (2630ft/802m) the highest summit, before dropping steeply over the rocky Prison Band before climbing again to Wetherlam (2502ft/762m). The route from Wet Side Edge to Wetherlam is a fine ridge traverse and more than makes up for its undulating path.

From the summit of Wetherlam, it is worth noting the rest of the route because the path climbing out of Greenburn Beck to reach Rough Crag is not easy to see once the descent is made and it is easier to note its position before completing the descent. As for the descent, there are several paths down to the beck, all of which arrive at or near the old mine workings.

Weatherlam from Hodgett's Close, near Coniston

From Greenburn Beck, search for the best path up to Rough Crags from where a clear path can be followed back towards Wet Side Edge from where a descent to Wrynose Pass can be made.

42. Stanley Ghyll and Hartley Crag

Stanley Ghyll possesses a fine waterfall which is circumnavigated in this Eskdale route with the climb of Hartley Crag an optional extra.

Walking distance: 5ml/8km

Amount of climbing: 710ft/220m

How to get there:

By car: Car park at the start at Dalegarth (MR173007)

By train: Ravenglass and Eskale Miniature Railway between Ravenglass and Dalegarth.

Refreshments: Dalegarth railway station café.

Nearest tourist information: As above.

From car park turn right for 300yds to the Eskdale Centre. Here, go left, signposted to Dalegarth Falls and heading over River Esk before bearing left after further 200yds there is a signpost to "waterfalls". Follow track uphill and as it bears round to right go ahead through gate onto the wooded Ghyll path.

The path climbs up through Stanley Ghyll crossing it twice after which it divides where the left fork is taken, arriving at the edge of the ravine above the falls. From here a stile is seen leading to open countryside, cross this and take a grassy track (100yds on right), to reach Low Ground. At farm cross a stile onto an enclosed track and after 150yds take a track through a gate on your left to Whincop.

At Whincop, go through two wooden gates, bearing left round a building to reach a stile. Cross this and continue to reach a wall and stile. Here turn right for Hartley Crag. The route continues over rough ground due north to reach crossing a wall with a path running left between wall and beck. Follow this path downhill until beck heads sharp right, here go over wall to reach a stile from which a clear track leads to River Esk.

At crossing a track by river head right to reach stepping stones opposite church (bridge quarter of a mile upstream). Cross and follow the clear track to reach the road opposite Boot junction. Turn left for your car.

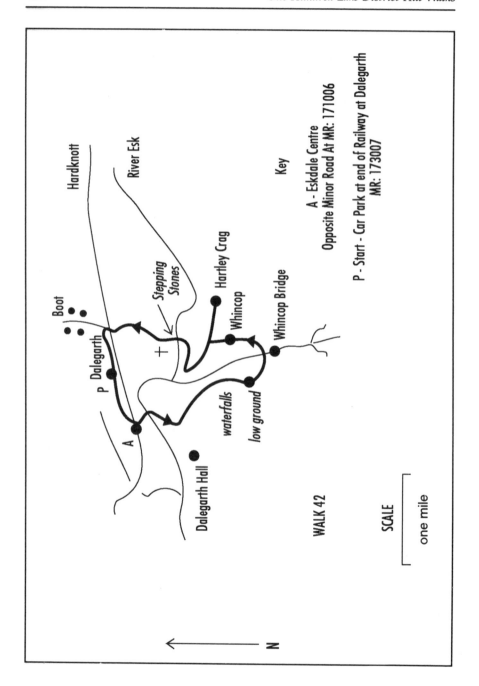

Hardknott

River Esk

Boot

Dalegarth

Stepping Stones

Hartley Crag

Whincop

Whincop Bridge

P

A

waterfalls

low ground

Dalegarth Hall

Key

A - Eskdale Centre
Opposite Minor Road At MR: 171006

P - Start - Car Park at end of Railway at Dalegarth
MR: 173007

WALK 42

SCALE

one mile

N

Stanley Ghyll

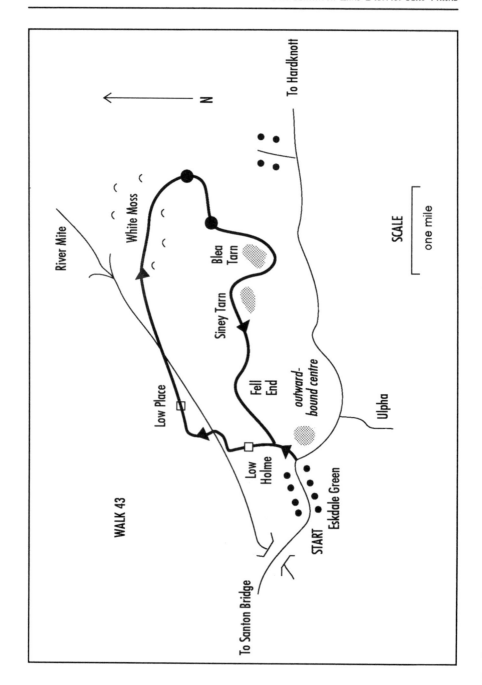

43. Mitredale and Bleatarn Hill

A short scenic route along a rarely visited dale followed by a fine ridge route with views of Eskdale.

Walking distance: 8.1ml/13km

Amount of climbing: 1160ft/360m

How to get there:

By car. Eskdale Green car park, next to the Outward Bound Centre (MR142002).

By train: Ravenglass and Eskdale Miniature Railway between Ravenglass (Cumbria Coast Line) and Eskdale Green.

Refreshments: King George IV Inn (MR149998). Shop, Eskdale Green.

Nearest tourist information: See Walk 44.

From the car park, pass the telephone box on the road bend and take footpath on left, signposted "Mitredale". Follow clear track uphill ignoring all other paths until it descends to a tarmac track at the edge of River Mite. Here turn right up the track, through the gate and over the river to reach Low Place.

At Low Place go through gate on right at the end of a farmyard, signposted "Wasdale". After 100yds take a footbridge on right to cross river and continue on the east bank eventually running along the edge of wood. At the end of the wood, go over stile and climb uphill to reach a stile on the edge of open fell land.

Here an indistinct path heads left contouring round White Moss before descending to derelict barns south east of the high ground of Brown Band. (A direct route over the moss is only possible in dry weather). From these barns on the Eskdale side of the ridge, a clear grassy track heading uphill past fenced off mine shafts can be followed to Bleatarn summit (938ft/290m).

From the summit follow the path downhill on the left of Blea Tarn. At the end of the tarn turn sharp right on a narrow track leading uphill to Siney Tarn. Follow the path round the tarn before heading west-south-west towards Fell End and Mitredale woods. Although this track is easily missed, all paths lead to edge of woodland. At woodland follow the boundary on clear paths round Fell End and through a clearing to reach a gate at the edge of the Outward Bound Centre. Go through this and onto track leading back to the car.

Miterdale

44. Esk Pike and The River Esk

This route follows the River Esk from its gently flowing path along the Esk valley to the river's source at the head of the valley, an area dominated by Esk Pike. It is a straight forward route with no navigational problems but can be wet underfoot particularly around Great Moss.

Walking distance: 13ml/20.8km

Amount of climbing: 2800ft/854m

How to get there:

By car. Car parking can be found on the grass verges near the entrance to Brotherlikeld Farm (MR212011).

By train: Two and a half miles walk between start and Dalegarth on the Ravenglass and Eskdale Miniature Railway.

Refreshments: Dalegarth Railway Station café; Woolpack Inn; Burnmoor Inn (Boot); Greendale Guest House.

Nearest tourist information: Dalegarth Railway Station café.

From the farm entrance follow the track over Hardknott Gill before heading left round the farm buildings on a path running alongside the River Esk. The route continues upstream on the east bank passing several deep pools which are frequently used for swimming to reach Lingcove Bridge a couple of miles later. Here fork left to reach Great Moss. If this area is particularly wet the west bank of the river provides a drier path or alternatively the higher ground of Great Crags will allow the area to be avoided completely. Whichever way is chosen, the path soon starts to climb to Lakeland's highest pass at Esk Hause from which the summit of Esk Pike (2903ft/885m) is easily reached.

From the summit descend towards Bow Fell to reach the low ground at Ore Gap. Here follow Yeastyrigg Gill downhill keeping to the east side as it heads towards Lingcove Beck. From here a short walk downstream leads to Lingcove Bridge where the track is followed back to the car.

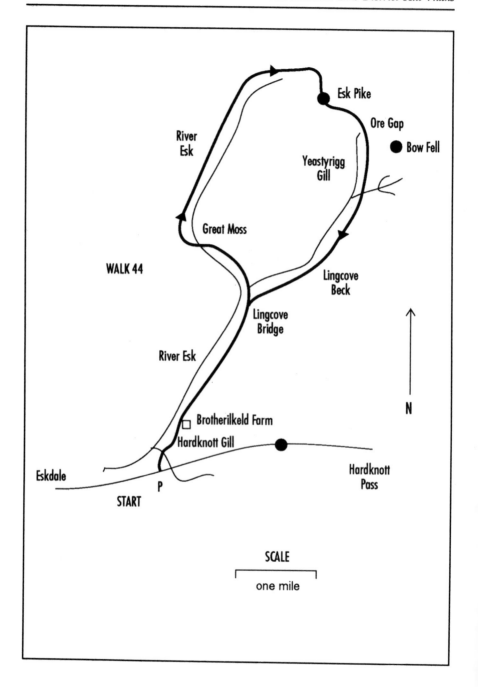

Esk Pike

Ore Gap

River
Esk

Bow Fell

Yeastyrigg
Gill

Great Moss

WALK 44

Lingcove
Beck

Lingcove
Bridge

River Esk

Brotherilkeld Farm

Hardknott Gill

Eskdale

Hardknott
Pass

N

P

START

SCALE

one mile

45. Yewbarrow

The ascent of Yewbarrow is a short, steep, spectacular climb that needs confidence to negotiate steep scree slopes to reach the summit, but for those able to achieve this, the effort is well rewarded.

Walking distance: 5ml/8km

Amount of climbing: 1900ft/580m

How to get there:

By car. Over Beck car park on the Wasdale Head road (MR168068).

Refreshments: Wasdale Head Hotel and farms.

Nearest tourist information: Barn Door Shop, Wasdale Head.

From the car park, walk alongside Over Beck to reach a clear path at the end of parking area that runs alongside the beck eventually arriving at a wall that rises up the main limb of Yewbarrow. There are paths on both sides of the wall of which either may be followed uphill to a point about 150yds below the crags of Bell Rib where a stile crosses the wall and a path heads north contouring the side of Yewbarrow heading direct to Dore Head.

Follow this path for 200yds towards Dore Head and look for the gap between Dropping Crag and Bell Rib. The wide gap is easy to find but is quite steep and scree covered and will lead the walker through the crags onto an easier gradient from where the summit (2058ft/628m) is easily reached.

From the summit follow the ridge to Stirrup Crag from where a zig-zag path leads down to Dore Head. Despite its name, Dore Head is the head of Over Beck and from here an easy descent along the west bank over Gosforth Crag Moss soon leads back to the car park.

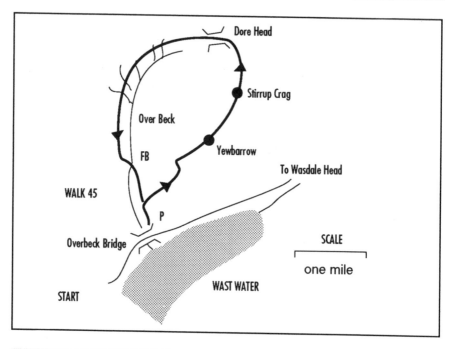

WALK 45

Dore Head

Stirrup Crag

Over Beck

Yewbarrow

FB

To Wasdale Head

P

Overbeck Bridge

SCALE

one mile

WAST WATER

START

Yewbarrow, in a coat of snow

46. Great Gable

The route up Great Gable is a classic walk almost entirely on steep rocky paths leading to the summit of one of Lakeland's best loved mountains.

Walking distance: 5.8ml/9.2km

Amount of climbing: 2700ft/820m

How to get there:

By car: The start of the walk is the unofficial car park a quarter of a mile south of Wasdale Head (MR187084).

Refreshments: See Walk 45.

Nearest tourist information: See Walk 45.

From the parking place follow the clear stony track signposted to Sty Head Pass towards Burnthwaite, passing a church on your left. At Burnthwaite, follow slate footpath signs to the left round buildings and through gate onto grassy area. Here turn right following clear bridleways towards Sty Head.

On crossing Gable Beck by a wooden footbridge, turn left by a cairn on a steep uphill path. This heads through a gate after 150yds to continue uphill in the same direction. At the scree line the path's gradient eases but continues to rise to Beck Head. Follow a track to the small tarn at Beck Head from where a path continues to the right, gradually ascending the north side of Great Gable. After 100yds, a track heads off to the right, leading to the summit (2949ft/899m). There are shorter routes to the summit via Great Napes but these all require considerable climbing on scree. The above route is the easier and more enjoyable alternative.

The summit is popular, large and flat and care should be taken to find the cairned route heading south-east to Sty Head. Once on the path it is easy to follow but loose rocks and scree make it difficult in places. From Sty Head, head right just before the Mountain Rescue box on what rapidly becomes a clear path descending down the south slope of Great Gable to reach our initial upward path.

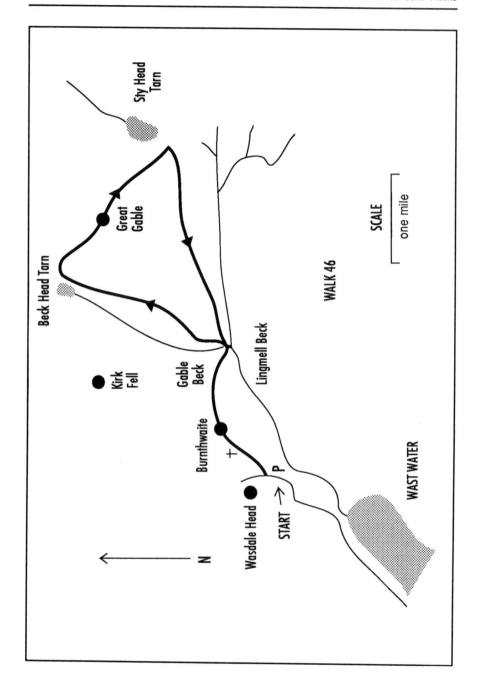

47. Scafell Pike via Piers Gill

The route chosen for the climb of England's highest mountain is a spectacular but less frequented approach to the summit avoiding the standard heavily eroded ascent via Mickledore. The route also includes a ridge walk along the summit skyline before returning on an easy gradual descent to Wasdale.

Walking distance: 9.3ml/13.9km

Amount of climbing: 3350ft/1022m

How to get there:

By car. The start of the walk is the unofficial parking green a quarter of a mile south of Wasdale Head (MR187084).

Refreshments: See Walk 45.

Nearest tourist information: See Walk 45.

From the parking area follow a stony track, signposted "Sty Head Pass to Burnthwaite". Turn left at a farmyard followed by right through a gate on the popular Sty Head path. Continue along bridleway until 200yds past Gable Beck. Here take the path running alongside Lingmell Beck, ignoring the main path heading up to Sty Head (this will be your descent).

Once on the beck path, continue uphill keeping the beck on your right until a major fork in the beck. Here, take a fork to the right, heading towards the crags below Lingmell. After a further quarter mile, cross another major tributary to find a clear path running up the east slope of Piers Gill. (NB. There is no path on the west bank and the Gill rapidly becomes a ravine which is impassable). From the path, the route alongside Piers Gill Ravine is easy to follow; this attractive route eith only a gradual and constant gradient of ascent, eventually arriving at a crossing track known as the Corridor Route. This clear path is followed right for 150yds before heading left on the cairned route to the summit (3210ft/ 978m).

The descent from the summit is easy once the correct path heading north east to Broad Crag has been found. The ridge is then followed to Great End from where the descent to Esk Hause (highest pass in the Lake District) is reached.

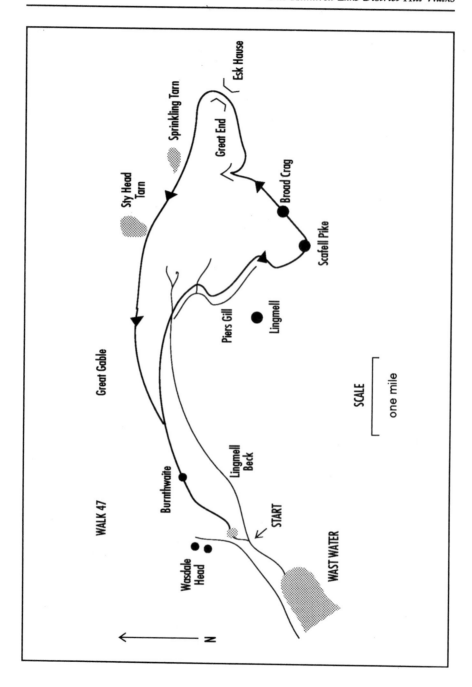

From this crossing point head north east for 150yds to reach a bridleway that links Langdale to Wasdale. Here head left downhill on clear popular track past Sprinkling Tarn and Sty Head Tarn to find the path to Wasdale Head starting to the left, just past the Mountain Rescue box on the summit of Sty Head. From this point Wasdale Head can be clearly seen at the foot of the path.

The very roof of England: the trig point and shelter on top of Scafell Pike.

Pike O'Blisco rises majestically in the Langdales

48. Pike O'Blisco

Pike O'Blisco (2304ft/705m) is a spectacular craggy summit with fine views of Langdale and beyond and can easily be climbed by the route shown below which provides an alternative to the longer and harder standard route from Langdale. As such it provides a relatively easy route which requires the minimum of effort.

Walking distance: 2.5ml/4.7km

Amount of climbing: 1100ft/336m

How to get there:

By car. Parking can be found at the summit of the Wrynose Pass (MR278028).

Refreshments: Eskdale and Langdale.

Nearest tourist information: See Walk 38.

For the sketch-map for this walk, see the map for walk 41 (page 116).

The walk starts from the Three Shire Stone, a few yards off the main road on the east side of the summit. The stone is at the boundaries of the three old counties of Lancashire to the south, Cumberland to the west and Westmorland to the east. Behind the stone and rising uphill is a peat track clearly visible leading up towards Red Tarn. Follow this track to reach the southern edge of the tarn. Here head right uphill to the clearly visible summit which is surrounded by a rocky outcrop.

From the summit, the descent is directly down the ridge back to the Wrynose Pass road via Black Crag. The route is short but can be lengthened by following Wrynose Beck down to the road where it passes underneath the road at Wrynose Bridge leaving a short road walk back to the car. The path here is unclear but after heavy rain the beck turns into several tiny waterfalls, making the detour a worthwhile experience.

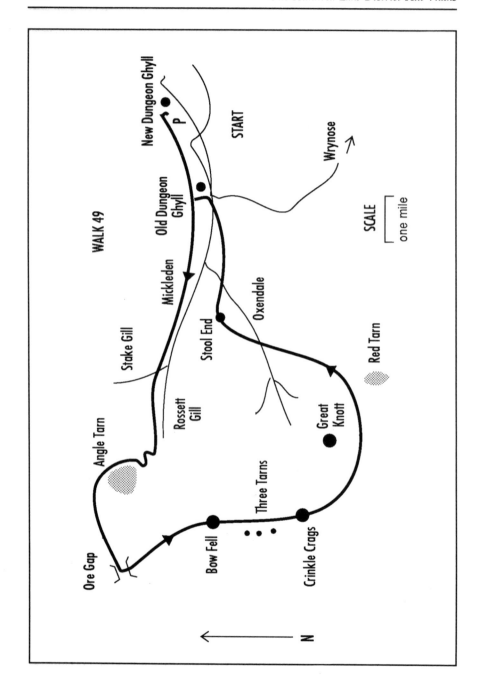

49. The Langdale Horseshoe

The Langdale Horseshoe is a tough circuit over the high crags dominating the head of the Langdale valley. The two main peaks of Bow Fell (2960ft/902m) and Crinkle Crags (2816ft/859m) are distinct summits in their own right with the latter comprising five separate summit tops. The paths everywhere are straight forward though a small amount of scrambling is necessary over Crinkle Crags.

Walking distance: 14ml/22.4km

Amount of climbing: 3750ft/1130m

How to get there:

By car. The start is at New Dungeon Ghyll car park (MR288060).

Refreshments: See Walk 38.

Nearest tourist information: See Walk 38.

From the car park, go behind the toilet block to reach the bridleway running alongside a wall heading up the valley. Follow a clear track past the Old Dungeon Ghyll onto what soon becomes the wide grassy area of Mickleden. After a further 1.5 miles the path crosses Stake Gill to head up Rossett Gill and climbs a zig-zag sequence of steps to reach a plateau above the valley with Angle Tarn lying in a hollow.

Head past the tarn and look left for an easy climb to reach the Esk Pike – Bow Fell ridge at Ore Gap. From here the ascent of Bow Fell is straight forward.

Descend from the summit to Three Tarns from where the path climbs up towards Crinkle Crags. This section requires care especially when descending from the highest point as the path drops vertically at one point requiring a scramble to get down and could be very dangerous in mist. However, once negotiated, the reward is a clear grassy slope reaching towards Great Knott before turning left steeply downhill prior to reaching Red Tarn. The track here is wide and popular as it descends to Oxendale, crossing the beck to reach Stool End from where the track is followed to the Old Dungeon Ghyll Hotel where the route rejoins the outward path.

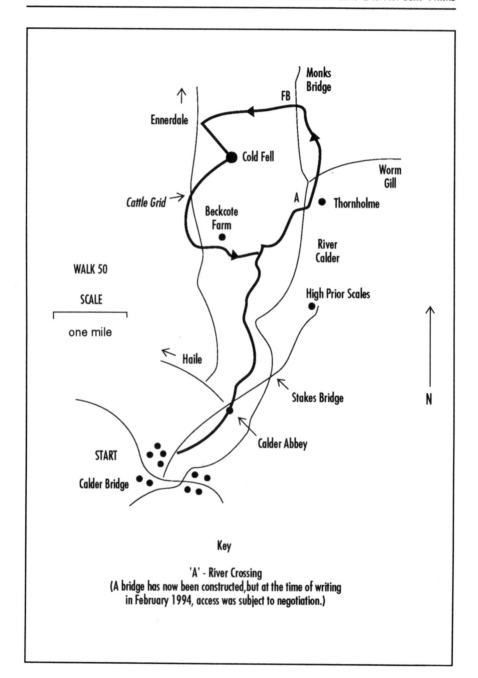

Key

'A' - River Crossing
(A bridge has now been constructed, but at the time of writing
in February 1994, access was subject to negotiation.)

50. Cold Fell and the River Calder

A low-lying route up the rarely-visited Calder Valley. The walk includes a river crossing which can be very difficult after heavy rainfall.

Walking distance: 7.5ml/12km

Amount of Climbing: 1470ft/450m

How to get there:

By car: Village Hall car park behind the church in Calder Bridge (MR042061).

By bus: Infrequent CMS bus service Whitehaven – Seascale passes through Calder Bridge.

By train: Sellafield or Seascale (Cumbria Coast Line). Then bus (from Seascale) or taxi (or cycle, and leave it at the garage near the Hall).

Refreshments: Public houses and Post Office/shop in Calder Bridge.

Nearest tourist information: See Walk 29.

From the church take the footpath signed to Stakes Bridge, passing behind Mill Garage and between houses to follow the track through fields towards Calder Abbey. This emerges on a minor road which is followed to a forestry track 50yds before Stakes Bridge.

Go along a signposted track and after 100yds head left uphill (signpost on right), to reach a stile at the entrance to open fields. Cross the stile and follow the field boundary round the next field to emerge at a double stile in the far right corner of field. Cross stiles and continue in same direction until a narrow strip of land with a clearly visible stile is seen on right. Go over this and after 50yds turn left to head downhill towards Thornholme.

At the river, look for telegraph poles crossing the river. Directly underneath, cross the river at a shallow point to reach a visible stile on the east bank*. Here follow the river upstream to reach the bridge over Worm Gill and a clear track. Follow track uphill before dropping to reach another bridge and track up to Cold Fell road. On the road, turn left for summit (955ft/290m).

---

*A footbridge has been built but, at the time of going to press, access over the bridge was still being negotiated.

From the summit descend to a cattle grid (MR053085) and follow the road, turning left for Beckcote Farm. On track, pass a house on the right and as the track heads left, go right through a farmyard, over a gate on the right to reach a wooden stile under an oak tree directly behind a farm. Here turn left crossing a further stile to reach the outward path.

Monks Bridge spans the River Calder

The North East

*This is covered by the North East sheet of
The English Lakes Outdoor Leisure
Ordnance Survey map.*

51. Aira Force, the Meldrums and Gowbarrow Park

One of the most popular and beautiful waterfalls in the Lake District, Aira Force rises to 70ft/21m. After that, an interesting round taking in Little and Great Meldrum and Swinburn's and Gowbarrow Parks, the latter a craggy expanse in the ownership of the National Trust, where William Wordsworth was inspired to write the poem that begins "I wandered lonely as a cloud".

Walking distance: 7ml/11.2km

Amount of walking: 975ft/300m

How to get there:

By car: Park in Aira Force public car park near toilets at the A5091-A592 junction on the banks of Ullswater (MR401201).

By bus: From Penrith.

Refreshments: Glenridding (MR387168)

There are several vantage points on this walk, which starts on the path north of the car park alongside Aira Beck. The path crosses the beck before the fall comes into view.

Our route continues over footbridges with the beck now on the left before reaching a lane opposite a farm. From the Ulcat sign, reach a T-junction and go right for 1ml/1.5km. At the next T-junction, on the Watermillock road, the turn is again right, for 1.5ml/2km.

Just past a caravan site on the left, take a waymarked path on the right. This goes over Priest Crag, Little Meldrum (1325ft/404m), Swinburn's Park, Kirksty Brow (1,200ft/360m), the National Trust fellside of Gowbarrow Park, Collier Hagg and Hind Cragg (820ft/250m) before joining another track. This meets up with Aira Force, from where steps are retraced to the car park.

Shortening the walk would detract from its enjoyment. However, if a short stroll is required, one from the car to Aira Force waterfall and back is rewarding (about 0.7ml/1km).

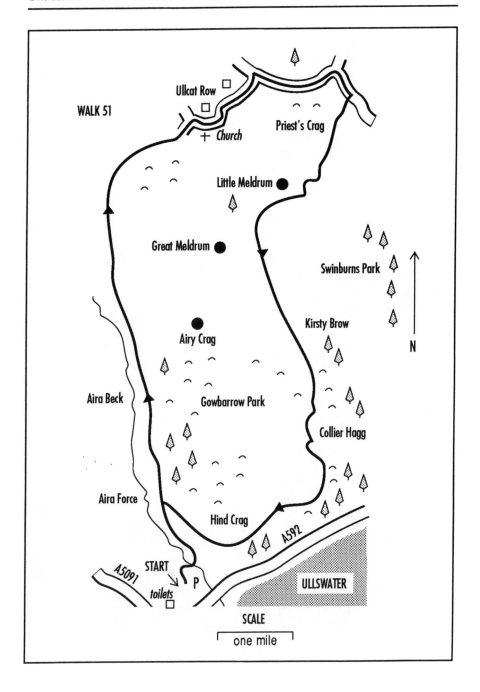

Aira Force in winter

52. Helvellyn

Extremely popular ascent from Wythburn on the western slopes. The start is pretty steep but walking becomes easy on the main ridge. Helvellyn, standing at 3116ft/950m, is England's third highest peak after Scafell and Scafell Pike.

Walking Distance: 2.3ml/3.6km

Amount of climbing: 2550ft/765m

How to get there:

By car: Good parking is available at Wythburn Church (MR325136) on the east side of the A591 five miles from Keswick. The park is right opposite the south end of Thirlmere.

By bus: Keswick-Lancaster service.

Refreshments: Thirlspot Hotel (MR316177).

Nearest tourist information: See Walk 1. Also Redbank Road, Grasmere. Telephone (05394) 35245.

A well-marked track heads through conifers beside a stream. A stile is crossed. The path zig-zags up to the open fellside. Parts of the trail are broken underfoot, but it improves dramatically on the main ridge. Almost 2000ft is climbed in the first mile.

The track leads over Comb Crags and on to the main ridge at Birk Side. Now it's easy all the way to the top. The last half mile is covered on a path which comes in from Dollywaggon Pike on the right. This is a real walkers' highway, broad and easy to follow.

Helvellyn's summit is quite austere, with a wall-shelter, trig point and two monuments. One, the Gough monument, was erected in 1890 as a tribute to a faithful dog which stayed beside its master's body for three months. The other smaller stone recognises the first aircraft landing on the plateau in 1926.

It's well worth looking over the summit rim to the famous and spectacular ridges on the eastern side. Striding Edge and Swirral Edge, either side of Red Tarn, are exciting ascents but not for the inexperienced. For many walkers the path from Wythburn is the safest bet, an easy way to the top of a friendly giant.

Looking up to Helvellyn from the banks of Thirlmere

The descent is best made on the same track. Three hours from top to bottom is an average time. Views of the Lake District are comprehensive as you would expect at this height.

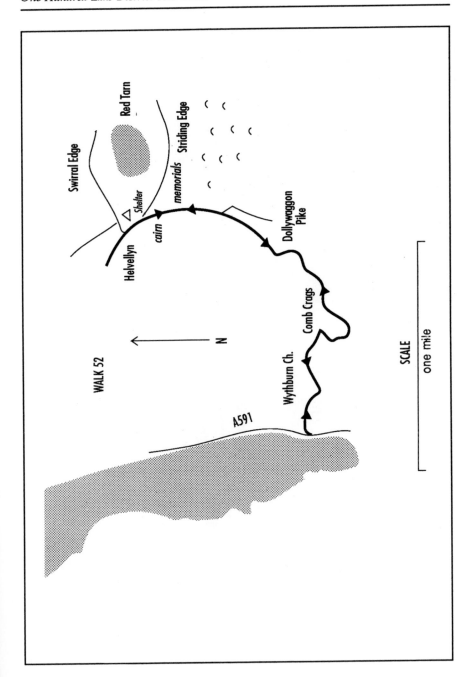

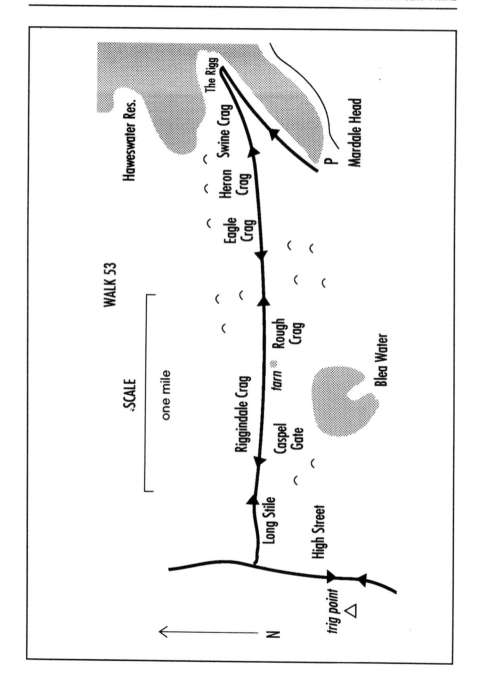

53. High Street

A classic route to the massive High Street plateau from the flooded valley of Mardale. It's a direct route with fine views all the way to the rim of a whaleback mountain top, standing at more than 2700ft.

Walking distance: 3ml/4.8km

Amount of climbing: 2050ft/625m

How to get there:

By car: Park at Mardale Head (MR469106).

Refreshments: Haweswater Hotel on Mardale Road.

Nearest tourist information: Robinson's School, Middlegate, Penrith, telephone (0768) 67466; The Square, Pooley Bridge, telephone (07684) 86530.

The road runs right along the edge of Haweswater, a reservoir for Manchester since the valley was swamped in the 1930s.

The path starts over the wall from the car park. Take note of the signpost and fork right from the straight-ahead track which leads to Nan Bield pass. A wooden bridge crosses Mardale beck. Now follow the flat trail along the lake edge for about half a mile.

Climbing begins in earnest when a sharp U-turn is made to the right before reaching a small plantation, The Rigg. The path is well-marked, if broken, all the way to the top, running beside and often dramatically-perched dry stone wall.

Soon after the turn is made the route straightens out and hits the summit ridge like a dart in a bullseye. Crags are close on both sides, with Swine Crag and Eagle Crag on the Riggindale flank.

At about 2000ft, the best of the walking begins, with the ascent of Rough Crag ridge. By now the wall has petered out. Rough Crag is followed by another little classic, the rocky stairway of Long Stile leading straight to the top.

Throughout the path is well-marked, though it cuts up badly in places in wet weather. A landmark between Rough Crag and Long Stile is Caspel Gate, a grassy depression with a small tarn.

An active walker could complete the climb in a couple of hours, but $2^1/_2$ to 3hrs would be average. Sadly, the summit does not live up to the approach; indeed, in mist it can be tricky as a proliferation of tracks is confusing. A trig point marks the highest point.

The High Street plateau

High Street, of course, is most famous as a Roman road. Legions tramped it on their way to Scotland and Hadrian's Wall. Horseraces have also been held on the great, flat plateau. On the descent, along the same route, take care where gradients are steep and the path is broken underfoot.

54. Fairfield

Fairfield, famous for its ten-mile horseshoe walk from Rydal to Ambleside, can also be approached from near Grasmere with easy access from the A591 Keswick road. Progress is easy up to about 2000ft. Then comes the sting in the tail, a hard pull from Grisedale Hause to the summit.

Walking distance: 3.75ml/6.03km

Amount of climbing: 2600ft/792m

How to get there:

By car: Parking is available in a layby near Mill Bridge (MR337092) on the opposite side of the road to the Traveller's Rest. Should this be full formal parking is available in Grasmere, half a mile to the south.

By bus: Keswick-Lancaster service.

Refreshments: Grasmere and Traveller's Rest.

Nearest tourist information: Grasmere (see Walk 52).

The real start to the walk is at Tongue Ghyll cottages. A signpost, marked Helvellyn and Patterdale, shows the way, firstly along a lane. Two gates have to be negotiated, the second leading to open fellside. The path up to this point follows Tongue Beck.

Then the beck splits and two routes are available. One follows Little Tongue Gill and the other, described here, runs up Tongue Gill on the right. It's easier and more interesting.

At about 1500ft, the path moves away from the beck and crosses a rocky outcrop. Cairns lead the way into a stony gully with a cascade. There's a natural tendency to stray into the scree on the left, so stick rigidly to the path. A giant cairn is the landmark before a hole in the wall leads through to Grisedale Tarn.

To the north of the tarn a zig-zag path leads to Dollywaggon Pike. To the right is the scree-strewn path to Fairfield. This is quite a tough scramble and should not be attempted in mist, though a broken wall is a guideline for part of the way.

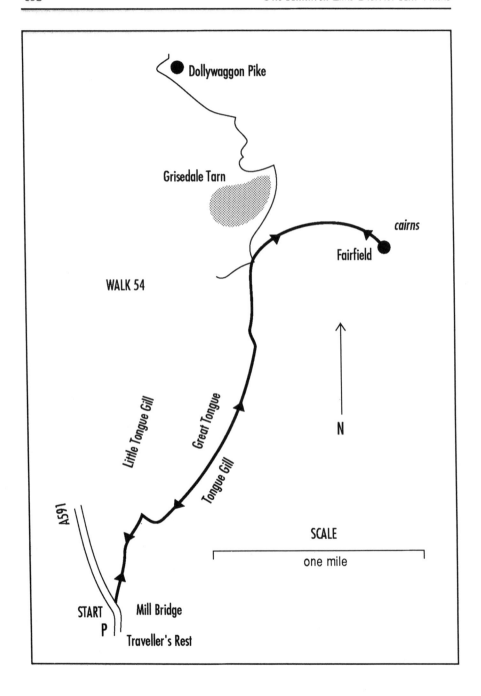

Dollywaggon Pike

Grisedale Tarn

cairns

Fairfield

WALK 54

N

Little Tongue Gill

Great Tongue

Tongue Gill

A591

SCALE

one mile

START

P

Mill Bridge

Traveller's Rest

At one point the path leads across the scree but keep going straight up. Fairfield, at 2800ft/665m is a superb top with fine ridges.

Again, it has to be stressed that it is a confusing place to be in mist. On a clear day, though the whole of the Grisedale Valley can be viewed, with Helvellyn and Striding Edge on the left.

If the weather deteriorates while the walk is in progress, turn back at the top of Tongue Gill. Time taken can range from $2^1/_2$ hours to more than four hours depending on fitness.

Members of Whitehaven Rambling Club on Fairfield

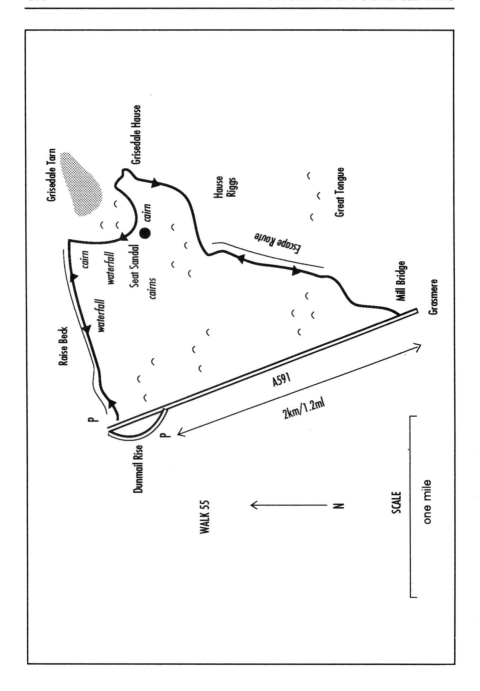

55. Seat Sandal

A quick, direct walk, ideal for the motorist who wants to stretch his legs. Seat Sandal is a mountain with no vices or surprises with easy access straight off the A591 Keswick-Ambleside road. It is, however, a fine viewpoint.

Walking distance: 3ml/4.8km

Amount of climbing: 1700ft/518.6m

How to get there:

By car: Leave the car as near as possible to the start from Dunmail Raise (GR328117).

By bus: Keswick-Lancaster service (CMS).

Refreshments: See Walk 54.

Nearest tourist information: Grasmere (see Walk 52).

A rough track can be picked out from Raise Bridge on the left side of the road coming from Keswick. It follows the beck of the same name right up the flank of Seat Sandal.

A sharp right turn is made above the second of two waterfalls. This leads straight to the summit, though the path is ill-defined. Seat Sandal's summit is flat and grassy, with small outcrops of rock breaking the monotony. Consolation for a rather dull climb comes in the views to west Lakeland. Giants like Scafell Pike, Great Gable and Pillar are there in all their glory. It is also possible to pick out a host of lakes and tarns.

Seat Sandal stands at 2415ft/736m and, from Grasmere, makes an imposing mark on the landscape. It is also possible to climb from Mill Bridge further down the A591 just above Grasmere. This route follows Tongue Gill and Grisedale Hause. The most imposing feature of Seat Sandal, Gavel Crag with its fine arete, looms up on the right.

This route is rather longer than the one from Dunmail Raise and partly overlaps with trails to Fairfield and Dollywaggon Pike. Seat Sandal is really just a leg-stretcher.

An escape route in bad visibility leads down to Grisedale Hause. A broken wall acts as a guide to safety and well-marked paths take the walker down to Grasmere.

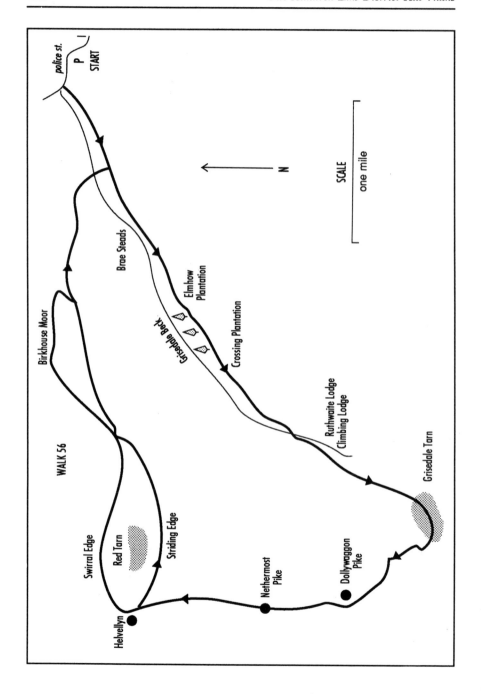

police st.

P

START

SCALE
one mile

N

Brae Steads

Elmhow
Plantation

Grisedale Beck

Crossing Plantation

Birkhouse Moor

Ruthwaite Lodge
Climbing Lodge

WALK 56

Grisedale Tarn

Swirral Edge

Red Tarn

Striding Edge

Nethermost
Pike

Dollywaggon
Pike

Helvellyn

56. Dollywaggon

Dollywaggon Pike is the southern sentinel of the Helvellyn range. It can be climbed as a one-off from Grasmere, Patterdale or Dunmail Raise. But a traverse of the ridge to Helvellyn is much more enterprising. However, the popular trail from Patterdale via Grisedale Tarn is a foolproof way up.

Walking distance: 6ml/9.65km

Amount of climbing: 2400ft/747m

How to get there:

By car: Park opposite Ullswater Hotel, Glenridding (MR387169) or in a lay-by at Grisedale Bridge (MR391162), opposite police station, Patterdale.

By bus: From Penrith.

By Ullswater steamer: Pooley Bridge – Glenridding.

Refreshments: Patterdale and Glenridding.

Nearest tourist information: Pooley Bridge. Telephone (07684) 86530.

Walking starts on a narrow road on the left bank of Grisedale Beck. It filters out into a bridleway, the trail passing Braesteads, Elmhow plantation and Crossing Plantation. Three miles or so from Patterdale a footbridge crosses the beck. A good landmark is the climbing hut at Ruthwaite Lodge. From here the gradient steepens, reaching about 2000ft at Grisedale Tarn. But all the way the path is well-defined.

To the north of the tarn a deep zig-zag track runs up the slope of Dollywaggon. It actually skirts the summit, so a small detour needs to be made to the grassy dome of the 2888ft mountain.

Now the view. To the north are the crags of Nethermost Cove and an aspect all the way to Helvellyn. The ridge continues to Nethermost Pike and on to Helvellyn itself less than two miles from Dollywaggon.

The walk can be turned into a full round by following the ridge then descending Helvellyn by one of the classic ridges, Swirral Edge or Striding Edge. Continue over Birkhouse Moor and back to Patterdale.

But many walkers may prefer to return by Grisedale Hause. Even this takes on a new dimension as Patterdale sweeps into view. It is also the safe way off if conditions deteriorate.

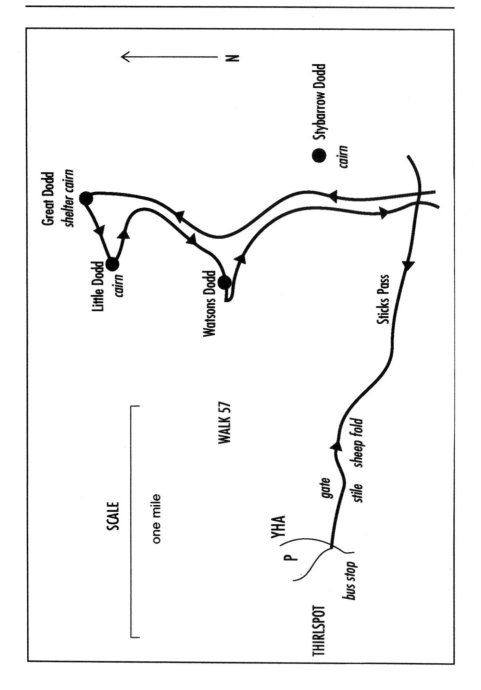

57. Great Dodd, Watson's Dodd, Stybarrow Dodd and Little Dodd

Nods with the Dodds over Sticks Pass, the second highest Lakeland Pass and a bracing walk thrown in. Tremendous views of Helvellyn, Blencathra and Thirlmere Lake make the climb worthwhile.

Walking distance: 9ml/15.3km

Amount of climbing: 2893ft/857m

How to get there:

By car: Park on the Keswick side of the A591, a few yards before the junction with the B5322 Threlkeld road (MR318189).

By bus: Keswick-Lancaster (see CMS timetable), to and from Thirlmere YHA.

Refreshments: Thirlspot Hotel (MR316176).

Nearest tourist information: See Walk 1.

A short path leads from the lay-by to the Threlkeld road, where a bridleway signed Glenridding and Sticks Pass takes you past the village hall and the right-hand Stybeck Farm track over a ladder stile.

Through a gate with a stile, climb left through another small gate. Slightly right, veer left with a Grasmere and Swirls permissive footpath sign on the right, which you do not follow.

Beyond the sheepfold, climbing stops for a while as you start on a flat stretch of the Sticks Pass (2420ft/746.2m), on 150 degrees south east for about a mile to a four-way junction of paths, before which there is a nice glimpse of Thirlmere over the right shoulder.

At the junction, go left (north) to reach the cairn on top of Stybarrow Dodd (2756ft/848m), your first nod with a Dodd.

Over Deepdale Crag, by-pass Watson's Dodd to the left, for the time being, and climb just over 200 feet (about 70 metres) to the turning point and main goal of the walk, the shelter (possible lunch stop) on Great Dodd summit (2807ft/857m).

Two tracks run almost parallel at this point. Keep to the dirt-covered one. From the shelter and cairn on top of Great Dodd follow a 360 degrees NW bearing to the next cairn, where a left turn is made on 230 degrees SW to Little Dodd (2451ft/780m).

At the Little Dodd junction, the Clough Head-Calfhow Pike-Millgil Head path is taken left to the next turn right, to the cairn on Watson's Dodd (2564ft/789m), where the way is right (140 degrees south-east) back to one of the two parallel paths.

Stybeck Farm at the start of Sticks Pass

Here is a right turn, but looking left you can see the Great Dodd shelter rising high above everything else around. Passing a cairn with a piece of green slate seen on the outward journey, on Deepdale Crag, it is not far now past a pile of stones to the Sticks Pass junction, which is near an oddly shaped small tarn.

The climbing is over. Follow a left-hand beck for a while before reaching the sheepfold again from where it is all downhill to a small gate with "No path" written on it. Here go right for a few yards and through the next small gate, a right-hand stile and ladder stile over a wall to wind past a farmstead and return to the car or bus.

58. Barton Fell and Arthur's Pike

A light walk with slight gradients at the lower end of Roman road High Street with bird's eye views of Ullswater, nine miles long and the second largest lake after Windermere in the Lake District.

Walking distance: 8ml/12km

Amount of climbing: 1125ft/350m

How to get there:

By car: Pooley Bridge car parks either side of Ullswater Bridge on the B5320 road (MR470244).

By bus: CMS bus from Penrith.

Refreshments: Pooley Bridge.

Nearest tourist information: Pooley Bridge 86530. The Square.

From wherever you park or get off the bus, walk through Pooley Bridge village and along a right-hand lane between St Paul's Church and Elm House. A Howtown, Martindale and caravan site signpost leads you over cross roads following a rising cul-de-sac lane signed Roehead.

A few yards past Roehead Farm, go through a small gate at the side of a larger one marked Barton Fell Common. You are now on open fell on the bridleway to Helton. The slight gradient continues beyond a grassy crossing just before the crown of the track, to reach a cairn and a four-way signpost, where the way is right along a bridleway pointing to Howtown and the Roman road. Keep on the broader of two tracks, maintaining height along a route where you will normally meet wild ponies. Swinging right over a ford, take a left fork after a few yards. In a few more yards, fork right and at a cairn follow another right fork, making sure you do not drop towards Ullswater.

Ignore a broad green track dropping right and continue towards the wood. Keep ahead where another broad track dips right and stride Aik Beck. At cross tracks, go left (opposite to the track with an iron gate). This juncture is Barton Park and the route now being embarked upon takes you over Barton Fell.

The first prominent feature is White Knott, a small outcrop on the right.

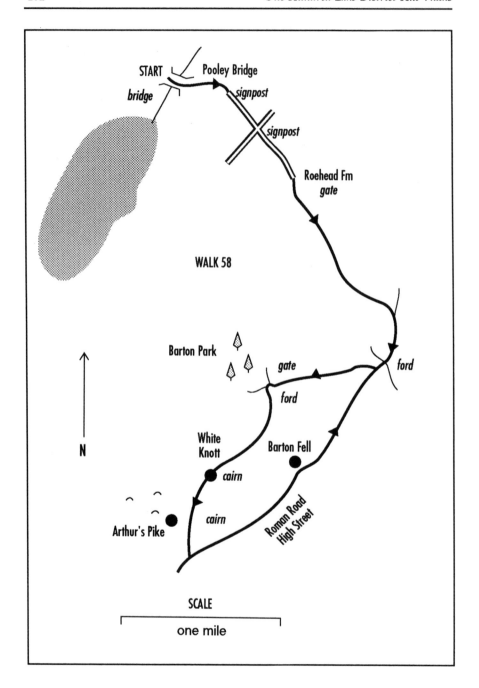

Continue on the steadily rising track over one cairn and on the next cairn on Arthur's Pike (1650ft/510m). This is the highest summit on the walk, which is comparatively easy from now on, although you will go over some wet land.

Soon the T-junction with High Street is reached. Take a left turn on 40 degrees north-east and continue for just under two miles with a fine view of Ullswater down left, to a familiar junction and a short right turn to tackle the ford encountered on the outward journey. It is now a matter of reversing that track, as the bridleway bends left to the four-way bridleway sign. Left now back through the gate near Roehead Farm, a host of golden daffodils in springtime. You hit the tarmac again and go over the cross roads at the Pooley Bridge boundary sign and left at the church to return to the village.

Fell ponies on the trek above Ullswater

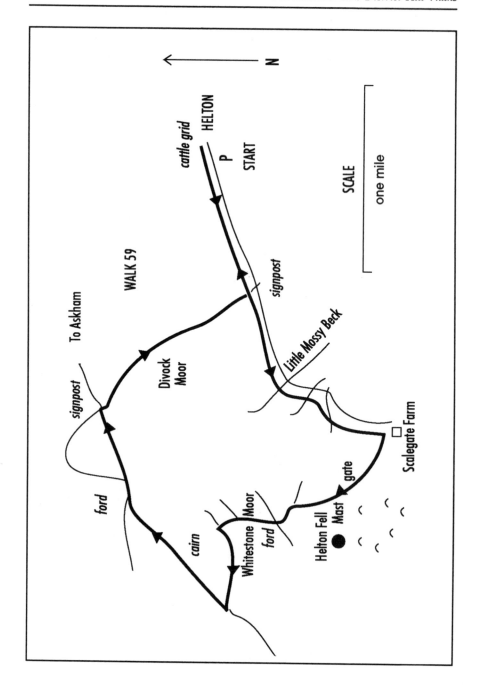

59. Helton Fell

Fell ponies and the sight of pony trekkers, also the customary sheep, are features of this quiet stroll on a little walked side of Ullswater and High Street.

Walking distance: 5.6ml/8.5km

Amount of climbing: 516ft/159m

How to get there:

By car: Park on left just over cattle grid on the fell road above Helton village. From Askham direction take first right after the boundary sign (at B & B signs), then next right (MR508219).

Refreshments: Village store; public house, in Helton.

Nearest tourist information: See Walk 53.

Continue along the fell road with Outgang Farm on the right and a rookery on the left. There was the sound of the curlew as photographer Bill and I were just in time to see a shepherd guiding his flock with the help of two dogs. This is part of the Lowther Estate, the family seat of the Earls of Lowther, Lowther Hall, being less than two miles north east.

Across the Bampton-Pooley Bridge bridleway, the fell road bends left over Little Mossy Beck and tributaries.

Over a cattle grid at a Lake District National Park bridleway notice, take a grassy track right, just before Scalegate Farm. Now comes the first real climb, over The Knotts, Helton Fell and Whitestone Moor.

On the fell summit is a mast, which is on the left after passing through a wooden gate on a right fork. The walk develops into an undulating stroll with a left turn at the next track and a right one over a ford at the next broad track.

Take a left fork a few hundred yards up and turn left on the next track 280 degrees due west. A further jaunt over the moor in this direction leads to the course of the Roman road known as High Street. This is at the lowest end of the Street, but at its highest point it rises to 2718ft/828m.

On the Street, turn right (north east) towards a cairn and the wooded

Heughscar and Skirsgill hills ahead. A first glimpse of Ullswater comes into view down and, over to the left, below the watchful eye of Dunmallard Hill, also wooded.

After walking between Ullswater and the last two mentioned hills reach a cross track and go right across a ford to a cross-ways sign where the way ahead is to Askham.

Turn right, however, on the Helton pointer. Keep on the track over Moor Divock, scene of small stone circles, ring cairns and barrows, to the sign on Helton Fell road and a left turn back to the car.

Note: One of the Moor Divock circles was excavated in 1866, when a Yorkshire-type food vessel was found.

Sheep gathering at Helton

60. Askham Fell and Heughscar Hill

As on the last ramble, wild fell ponies are again a feature as a trek is taken from the attractive large village of Askham. Over Askham Fell, ideal country for local pony trekkers, the Pooley Bridge-Helton bridleway is reached. The other side of Heughscar Hill and the magnificent view point of Heugh Scar is the hamlet of Celleron, from where a pleasant country lane returns you to Askham.

Walking distance: 5.3ml/9km

Amount of climbing: 546ft/168m

How to get there:

By car: In Askham, take Pooley Bridge bridleway (marked cul-de-sac) almost opposite the Post Office (the turn opposite the Lowther Park junction) and park in space on the fell road just short of a cattle grid (MR509236).

Refreshments: Public house and Post Office in Askham.

Nearest tourist information: See Walk 53.

Proceed up the fell road with a stone building on the right. A right fork of ways leads towards a small wood mapped as Riggingleys Top near an ancient settlement. Through a gate and along a carpet of short grass reach a junction where you have to make sure a left turn is taken on a 230 degrees south-west bearing, to go over Askham Fell, otherwise you will go careering on to reach the Heughscar Hill track too early.

At Ketley Gate cross-tracks follow the Pooley Bridge sign and go right at the next signed cross-ways towards Celleron, over Heughscar Hill and finding the limestone outcrop of Heugh Scar (1105ft/340m) a good place, perhaps, for lunch, with a brilliant view across Ullswater.

From here it is essential to take a 360 degrees bearing north, for the way is tricky, there being no clear track over boggy ground towards Winder Hall Farm. The route skirts the right-hand far corner of a dogged-leg plantation and keeps the farm on the right before continuing along a farm track to reach the lane near Celleron opposite a disused quarry.

A walk along the lane for just over a mile takes you back to Askham, the fell road and the car.

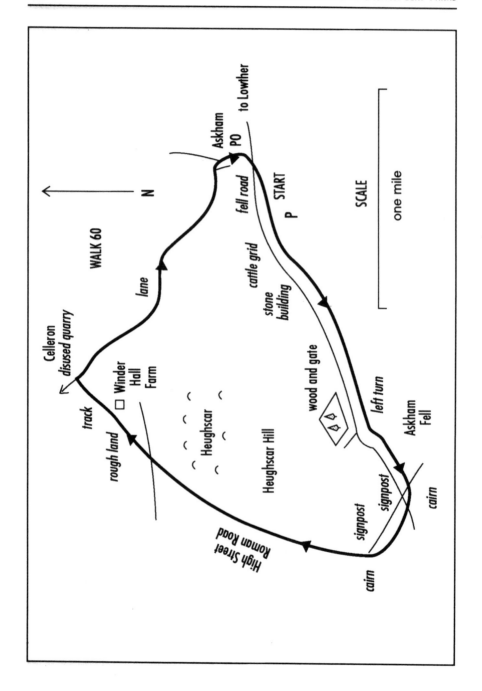

61. Knipe Moor

A delightful stroll along a bank of the River Lowther leads in less than a mile to a higher degree of adventure in crossing a rickety Bailey-type bridge. Then follows the more exacting exercise to the top of Knipes Scar, a climb rewarded with fine views over East Cumbria. I am afraid, however, that an extensive search among the limestone outcrop for a mapped stone circle proved negative.

Walking distance: 4ml/6km

Amount of climbing: 552ft/170m

How to get there:

By car: From Bampton travel on the Shap road towards Bampton Grange. Find parking space on the verge just over Haweswater Beck bridge (MR518181).

Refreshments: Crown and Mitre Inn (Bampton Grange); Post Office/store (Bampton).

Nearest tourist information: See Walk 53.

Back over the bridge, follow the right-hand footpath sign, for a few yards by a wood and Haweswater Beck and then alongside the meandering River Lowther, which has come from Keld Dub and is travelling in your direction towards Lowther Castle, ancient family seat of Earls of Lowther and Lords Lonsdale from the 13th century until 1936, when they moved to nearby Askham Hall.

Over the already noted bridge, climb a portion of Knipe Moor at left angles to reach the fell road near a telephone box. Turn right passing 16th century Knipe Hall and about 100 yards beyond the High Knipe farm road, start following the grassy tracks uphill to the summit of Knipe Scar.

On top, try and outdo me and search for the stone circle by all means. It is mapped to the left, but the way of the route is right to eventually follow the walled Inscar Plantation. Look carefully for a half-size gate and leave it downhill on 253 degrees south west, joining a track skirting High House and via Low Scarside to join the Shap road.

A right turn is the way through Bampton Grange, with the Crown and

Mitre opposite the church. Over the bridge spanning the River Lowther, go right at the road junction to the car.

In an emergency, the Scar may be eliminated from the walk by following the fell road over the cattle grid back to Bampton Grange. This, however, takes much of the excitement out of the route.

Bampton Grange Church is worth a visit with its timber arcades and wall painting of nearby Mardale Church before the valley was flooded to facilitate Haweswater Reservoir, visited in other rambles in this book.

How the author got to the other side of the River Lowther

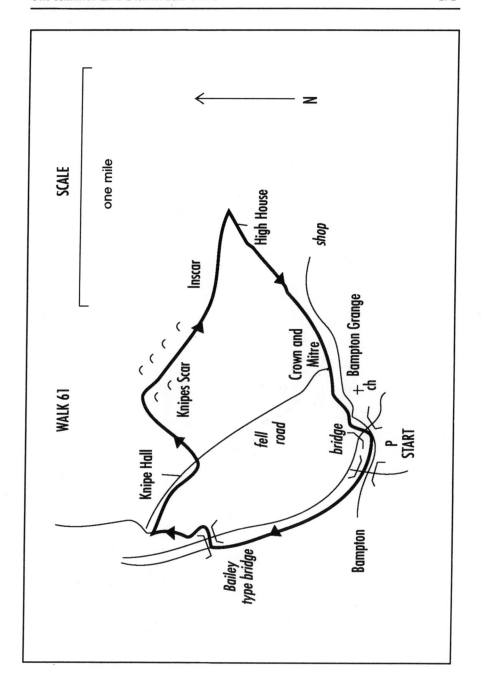

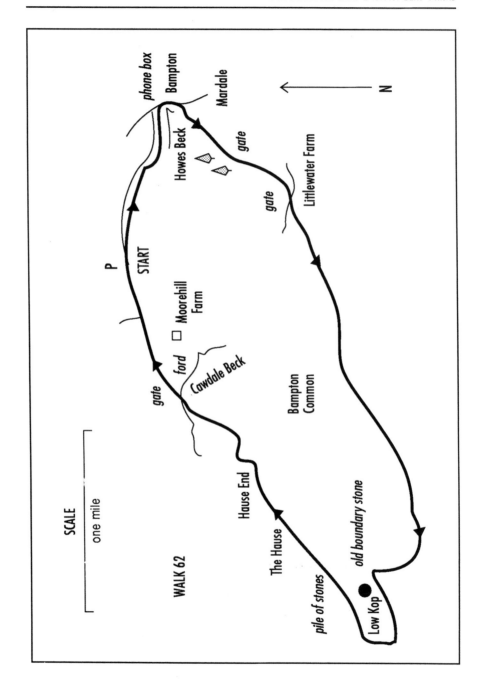

SCALE

one mile

WALK 62

N

62. Bampton Common

This walk is in the locality of the previous five rambles. As has been common with the other routes in this area, fell ponies are a feature. There is a bonus of a panoramic view of Haweswater Reservoir from the summit of Low Kop (1859ft/572m).

Walking distance: 6ml/10km

Amount of climbing: 1950ft/600m

How to get there:

By car: Park at MR500184. Approach along Hullockhowe fell road from Bampton.

Refreshments: St Patrick's Well Inn, Bampton; petrol filling station, Bampton; post office/store, Bampton.

Nearest tourist information: See Walk 53.

This undulating route is not as easy to follow as it looks on the map. Retrace steps along Hullockhowe fell road into Bampton, turning right at the telephone kiosk and bus shelter. Over Howes Beck Bridge on the Mardale road, look for a path starting at a wooden step stile and sign about 100 yards past St Patrick's Well Inn and just before a school sign.

Follow the track uphill on 230 degrees south west, head over a ladder stile, through a wall gap and over another ladder stile before going slightly diagonally left between trees and over a mound, maintaining the same compass bearing.

Along a footpath through grass and through a gate, turn left along a track onto a road at a gate and footpath sign. Go right for a few yards to a left-hand footpath just beyond the Littlewater "private" sign. Over the stile walk diagonally right to follow a wall and make for a ladder stile over the wall to the right.

A further walk through a meadow, a "bouquet" of wild flowers in season, takes you over another tree-topped mound to yet another ladder wall stile, this time near a barn.

A stone step stile in a wall gap is the next point of progression, after which a diagonally left turn swings along a track at the side of a farm. Take the direction of a "permissive path to fell" sign attached to a barn.

Through a gate and across a track make sure you are still following 230 degrees south west. With a farm down to the right there are several tracks, but take the extreme right fork now on 260 degrees south west.

You are now confronted with an undulating stretch of fell. On the last knoll before an extensive view of Haweswater is obtained, swing diagonally right across what is now Bampton Common. Keep a further cairn to the left and keep swinging slightly right over the remains of an old quarry onto Low Kop (1859ft/572m), the highest point of the walk to reach a junction of ways near an old boundary stone.

The turning point of the trek, this is a place to lunch and linger, enjoying the view of Haweswater. For the return jaunt, you must follow a path on a bearing of 85 degrees east. Dip and rise over a further hill with a pile of stones and along what is mapped as The Hause and Hause End. After the descent, the path is stony. Pass a ruin and ford Cawdale Beck, which can be deep after rain.

Through a gate at Moorahill Farm, follow the track 90 degrees east to reach tarmac and pass an old farm building and left-hand junction to return to the car.

Cawdale, near Bampton

63. High Raise

This is Golden Eagle country. During nesting time there is great anticipation among hundreds of observers hoping to catch a glimpse of Britain's premier bird and possible offspring. Riggindale, the centre of this route is its only breeding ground in England. Just off the route, the Royal Society for the Protection of Birds have an observatory where the public are welcome to use their telescopes.

Walking distance: 8ml/12km

Amount of climbing: 2275ft/700m

How to get there:

By car: Mardale Head car park at the end of Mardale road at the side of Haweswater Reservoir (MR469106).

Refreshments: See Walk 53.

Nearest tourist information: See Walk 53.

At the far end of the car park, leave through a wicket gate at the side of a farm access gate, along a stony track over a beck and follow the Bampton footpath sign.

The path swings right over Mardale Beck footbridge through a wicket gate and across two further footbridges, narrow and wide, to go along the lakeside to woods mapped as The Rigg.

Follow the bend in the lake to pass a stone barn on the well-trodden path to the eagle observation point. The stone wall here is the boundary of the eagle area in the Riggindale valley and after attempting a sighting, if it is nesting time, retrace steps to just beyond the stone barn along a path between trees, down steps and across a railed footbridge.

Then, pass over a small packhorse bridge near a waterfall. The path winds to a vague junction with a wire strand fence ahead. Move to the left, away from Haweswater, rising a few feet above the beck and crossing it at a convenient point as you aim for the high craggy summit of Kidsty Pike ahead on a 320 degrees north west bearing.

This takes you to the Coast to Coast route, where the way climbs right

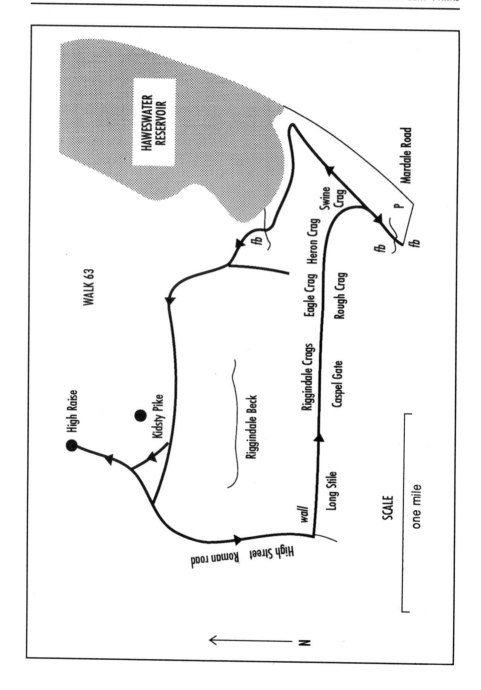

over Kidsty Hawes, over a stony and then peaty path before a left fork guides you to Kidsty Pike summit (2560ft).

From the top follow the 350 degrees north west bearing along a faint path which cuts off a corner towards the ultimate goal of High Raise (2634ft). For the mountain you reach the course of the Roman Road known as High Street and turn right.

High Raise is the turning point of the walk, half-way in mileage. Retracing steps along the Roman Road pass the junction you came out of and the next one and climb on a 180 degrees south bearing over Twopenny Crag.

On 190 degrees south west the idea is to keep on the main path towards High Street for a while, but I must admit I got mixed up with a sheep track where I had to turn left at another sheep track to rejoin the main path.

The next junction is clear as the path takes you over the enthralling Riggindale Crags for two undulating miles taking in Long Stile, Caspel Gate, Rough Crag, the aptly named Eagle Crag, Heron Crag and Swine Crag with the eagles having Riggindale Beck and valley all to themselves below.

Where a path crosses a wall to go up to High Street summit, keep on the left of the wall with a cairn on the left where the wall swings slightly right. Eventually move away from the wall and keep by the left-hand drop side of the ridge. Reach another cairn and bend left.

The stony path dips and as it starts to zig-zag, Riggindale Crags look down on Blea Water to the right. Take care because of erosion as you descend. The way is undulating and winding as you pass a small tarn. After an extensive drop, the path is again undulating.

Pass a tiny tarn over the right-hand wall. Go through a wall gap stile, then rise again – only to descend.

The ground is boggy as Haweswater comes into view. Head down a green slope towards Haweswater to the right onto a lakeside path, where a right turn takes you back to the car.

Allow about five hours.

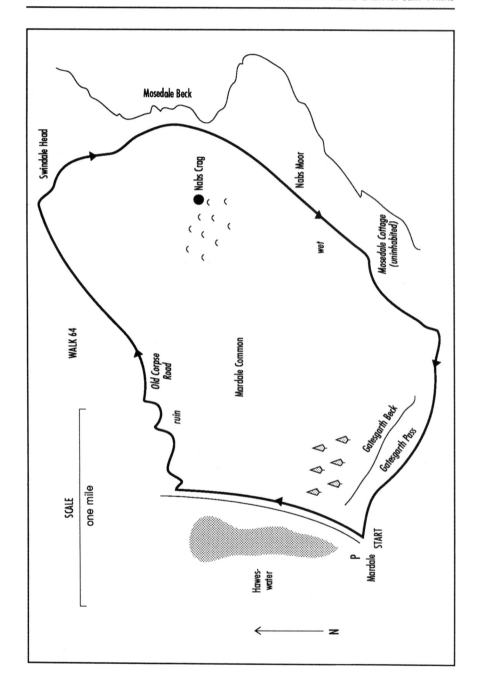

64. Mardale Common

This is a gruelling, undulating trudge through bog and mire. I counted three ruined buildings en route, though with me there were actually four ruins. Maybe it is not so bad if you start it fresh, but to save on time and petrol Bill and I did it immediately after the previous one – not to be recommended!

Walking distance: 8ml/12km

Amount of climbing: 2601ft/801m

How to get there:

By car: See Walk 63.

Refreshments: See Walk 53.

Nearest tourist information: See Walk 53.

Skirt Haweswater along the road for a mile over Hollow Stone bridge by the fall to follow the signed public footpath via the aptly named Old Corpse Road to Swindale.

Winding uphill towards the fall, the path bends at the first ruined barn of the walk and again at the second before a high point of a beck overlooking Swindale where Bill and I took water.

Continuing 75 degrees north east, turn right on a cross-path to a ladder stile and black gate. Fording a beck, traverse another black gate down to Swindale Farm (inhabited).

Through a gate marked with an arrow, follow Mosedale bridleway alongside a farm wall, over a step-stile at the side of a gate and along a stony lonning to pass through a little gate and a farm compound on 183 degrees south.

A further step-stile at the side of a gate takes you over a beck bridge. Rising slightly, the track runs parallel with Mosedale Beck and touches its bend at Simon Stone to continue on a cart track in the same direction. Now starts a winding climb over Nabs Crag and the wet and peaty Nabs Moor. There are parts covered in cotton grass.

Through a gate near the next ruin, Mosedale Beck flows down left (I just hope you have not crossed the tempting-looking bridge over Mosedale earlier on, otherwise you will be on the Way to Shap!)

On 260 degrees south west, eventually find the track which winds through a gate gap and over a ford towards Mosedale Cottages (uninhabited). Following the same bearing to the left of the cottages, start a hard climb over part of Selside Brow.

Continue over the energy-sapping moor, through a wooden gate and aim for a wall that looks like a bridge in the distance on the Gatesgarth Pass. At the junction with this, your way is right, up a stony track on a 340 degrees north-west bearing.

Ignore the left-hand track leading up to Little Harter Fell and then descend. Through a small National Park gate, drop towards woods and Haweswater to the right. In a few minutes you go down further past a sign post and through a kissing gate into the car park.

All in all, about four hours.

Haweswater

65. Glenridding Common and Helvellyn

Watch the sheep on Helvellyn! A few hungry ones gather round the shelter on the summit. They know where the food is, as the picture shows! After conquering the challenging ascent via the awkward Swirral Edge, you will need all the sustenance you can get.

Walking Distance: 8ml/12km

Amount of climbing: 3250ft/1000m

How to get there:

By car: Greenside Road car park, Glenridding (MR388169).

By bus: From Penrith to Glenridding.

Refreshments: Glenridding.

Nearest tourist information: Greenside Road car park. Telephone (07684) 82414.

Follow the Helvellyn sign out of the car park. A ranger service shed is on the right. Through the health centre grounds turn left on the road opposite The Stores. After passing the Travellers Rest on the right, go right at a junction and seat on the Greenside Mine-Keppel Cove sign. Follow the YHA at the bend.

Keep straight on from the cattle grid at Glenridding Common sign. High Rake Cottages are up to the right as you continue along the stony track. Eventually pass the YHA on the left and the notice board giving the handy telephone number of the Lake District National Park Weatherline (07687 75757).

Keep on the signs for Red Tarn and Helvellyn across a footbridge with an iron gate. Mires Beck flows to the right. Above the Weir, maintain a 245 degrees bearing north west. Catstye Cam (2892ft/890m) shortly rises right. A steady climb now starts over the tricky rocks of Swirral Edge and on to Water Crag. A 300 degree west bearing will take you along the path for Helvellyn summit (3087ft/950m), where there is the shelter to beware of the sheep and, nearby, a stone to commemorate the first landing of an aeroplane on a British mountain. Fix a 300 degree west bearing from the shelter to proceed to Lower Man, where the next

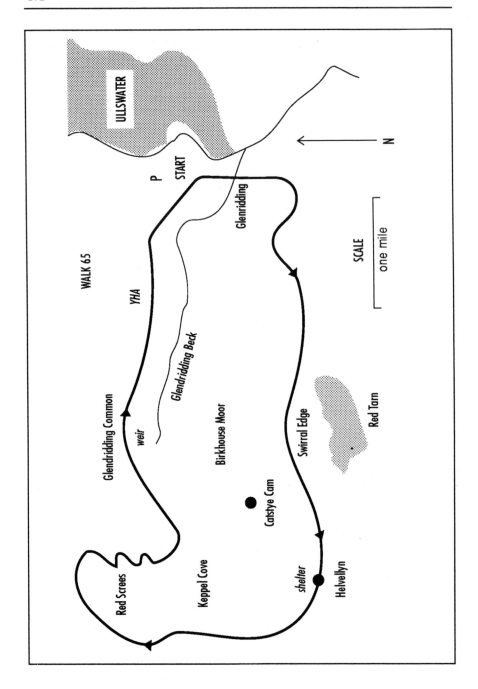

bearing should be 304 degrees north west. The next bit is hard to follow. The well-worn way splits, but where it splits needs to be detected carefully. On a bearing of 300 degrees north you follow the right-hand split. The left-hand one would take you down to Thirlmere. If in doubt, look across right from the nearest rise and observe a zig-zag path going down the fell side and then continuing alongside Glenridding Beck. The path, once you have established it, starts from Whiteside Bank and swings over Red Screes. Your bearing as the now unmistakable path starts its zig-zag way down should be 95 degrees north east.

At the beck-side turn left, over a wooden plank bridge and pass the Sticks Pass path coming in left. Round a right-hand bend, keep on the Glenridding path and once swinging left at Almond Lodge, you are on familiar ground.

Through the kissing-gate at the side of the cattle grid, reach the end of Greenside Road where the car park is diagonally right from Fairlight Guest House.

Allow just over five hours at a moderate walking pace, allowing a 20 minute lunch stop – sheep permitting, of course!

Striding Edge, Helvellyn

66. Great Rigg

This is a rare out-and-back walk in the book. It takes in Dunmail Raise, Grisedale Tarn, Seat Sandal and Fairfield before the turning point is reached on Great Rigg.

Walking distance: 7ml/10.5km

Amount of climbing: 2275ft/700m

How to get there:

By car: Lay-by near AA box and hostel on Dunmail Raise (MR327116).

By bus: Keswick-Lancaster (CMS) and National Express.

Refreshments: Grasmere.

Nearest tourist information: Grasmere.

From the ladder stile at the lay-by walk up the lower slope diagonally left, cross a dry beck and follow the shale path parallel with the main road. Go right up a stony track, steadily climb by the side of the babbling Raise Beck to a waterfall.

Looking back, Steel Fell and Dead Pyke can be viewed the other side of Dunmail Raise Pass. Seat Sandal (2392ft/736m) is right as you plod on. In front of Grisedale Tarn, turn right on the cross track, swinging round the lovely tarn on the way to Fairfield (2728ft/873m).

Over the next crossing path, reach the summit with two shelters and a cairn. Taking in the views of Windermere (ahead left) and Coniston (ahead right) with Elterwater between, set a bearing of 200 degrees south west. Great Gable and the Scafells are clustered among the mountains far to the right as you follow the bearing to dip and rise again onto Great Rigg (2554ft/786m). Take a well-earned rest before retracing steps to the main road. The way back to Fairfield, in case you have lost your sense of direction in mist, is on a 350 degrees north west bearing. At the shelter turn left on 280 degrees west, over rocks and scree again down to Grisedale Tarn. There is nearby "safety" grass if the scree seems uncomfortable.

From the tarn and Seat Sandal, the path is straight forward back to the start.

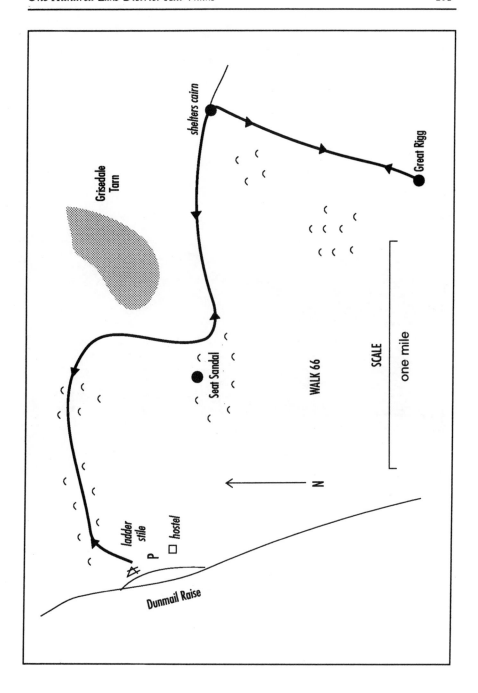

Griserdale Tarn

shelters cairn

Great Rigg

Seat Sandal

WALK 66

SCALE
one mile

N

ladder
stile

P □ *hostel*

Dunmail Raise

Great Rigg, part of the view of the Central Fells from Coniston

67. Dove Crag

Tricky crags are included in the hard-to-find outward route. Once firm paths are found beyond Stand Crags, the views are most rewarding.

Walking distance: 8ml/12km

Amount of climbing: 2600ft/800m

How to get there:

By car: Cow Bridge car park, Brothers Water (MR405133).

Refreshments: Brothers Water Inn, A592 (MR404118) and Sykeside caravan site (nearby) for shop and restaurant.

Nearest tourist information: See Walk 65.

Out of the car park to the right, near a Queen Victoria seat, pass through a gate and keep alongside the water. The path passes through a couple of gates and passes Hartsop Hall and farm buildings before a choice of ways for Dovedale, a fell path and a footpath.

Bill and I agreed to take the footpath. Bill thought maybe the fell path would have been better. As it turned out he was probably right. The footpath peters out after the Dovedale Beck crossing and waterfall. A compass bearing of 280 degrees west on the mapped path towards Dove Crag led us over tricky Stand Crags and Stangs before we eventually spotted a well-defined track running across our direction.

We made for this, the other side of a beck, and turned left. From picking up the mapped route, this appeared on viewing from a height to be the path from Brothers Water.

However, the way from now on should be straightforward. Left at a fence line which represents a civil parish boundary, Dove Crag (2574ft/ 792m) cairn is reached and shortly afterwards, a stone wall is followed as the way drops down a fence line left from a part-broken wall. Little Hart Crag is climbed. Because many paths vital to the walk appear to be unmapped, it is advisable not to look at the map at this stage; Brothers Water in the distance should be the goal and that is to the right when Scandale Pass is reached. With High Hartsop Dodd left, the path is the most straightforward of the ramble, on 40 degrees north east, over a stile and dropping further to an old barn. Pass through the precincts of this.

Follow the Patterdale and camp site sign, through a wicket gate and over a farm bridge. Right at the rear of the farm to pass through a left-hand small gate, go over a lattice bridge near a second farm. Keep left of the farmhouse on the familiar outward track through the gates and over the bridge back to the car park.

With all the "fun and games" you are likely to encounter, allow at least five hours.

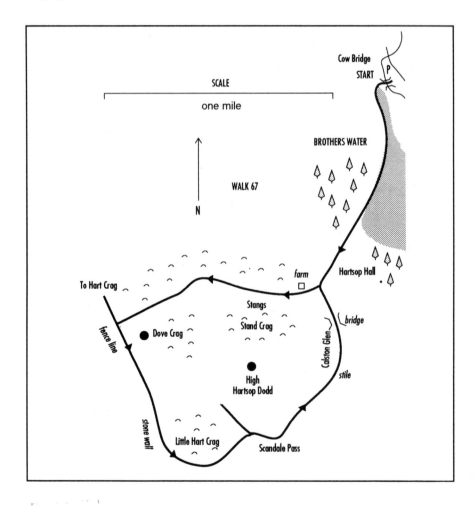

68. Hartsop Dodd and Stony Cove Pike

A climb of nearly 2000 feet gives great views of Kirkstone Pass, snaking its way between Windermere and Brothers Water. Allow four hours at average pace.

Walking distance: 4ml/7km

Amount of climbing: 1950ft/600m

How to get there:

By car: Park in lay-by on the Patterdale side of Brothers Water Inn on the A592 (Kirkstone Pass road) (MR404121).

Refreshments: See Walk 67.

Nearest tourist information: See Walk 65.

Opposite the Brothers Water Inn, go through an elevated National Trust wicket gate and turn right along a stony track to a wall where a footpath sign leads off the road at Caudale Bridge. Cross the beck and start to climb along a path which bends left and reaches a broken wall.

The path zig-zags towards the crag tops over loose scree, boulders, rocks, grass, ferns and bilberries. The faint track gets higher and higher above Kirkstone Pass. It is an exacting uphill scramble before reaching a welcome cairn with a cross atop. This is the summit of Stony Cove Pike (2479ft/763m).

There are two slate memorial plates on the cairn. One reads: "Hic Jacet. Mark Atkinson, of Kirkstone Pass Inn, died 14th June, 1930, aged 69 years". The other reads: "Also his son William Ion Atkinson, died 2nd April 1987, aged 83 years". You should have made this point in two hours. Because of the tricky nature of the terrain, it should take you the same time to get down.

For the return route, follow the wall ahead on a good path past a further cairn on a bearing of 345 degrees north west. You hop from one cairn to another. The well-worn way continues on the left of a wall. Ullswater comes into view in the distance.

The summit of Hartsop Dodd (1989ft/611m) is marked by the final cairn before you start dropping for the last time towards Hartsop Village.

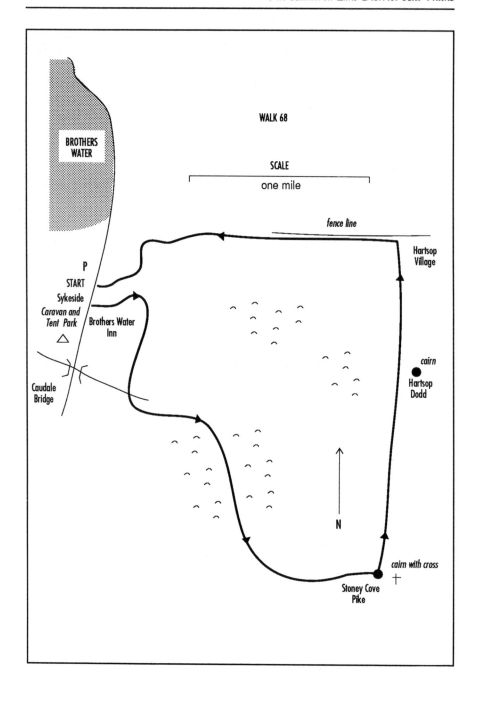

BROTHERS WATER

WALK 68

SCALE
one mile

fence line

Hartsop Village

P
START
Sykeside
Caravan and Tent Park   Brothers Water Inn

cairn
Hartsop Dodd

Caudale Bridge

N

cairn with cross
Stoney Cove Pike

When you eventually reach a footpath sign at a wire fence, the village, with car park and cattle mart, is down right, but your way is left alongside the fence. Brothers Water has by now come into view. The path leaves the fence and follows the edge of a low grassy cliff, descending gradually.

Turn left along the bottom fence, through the ferns and over a little bit of open fell above the trees, through which make your way down. Go through a gate onto the road and turn right for the car.

The summit of Stony Cove Pike with memorial cross

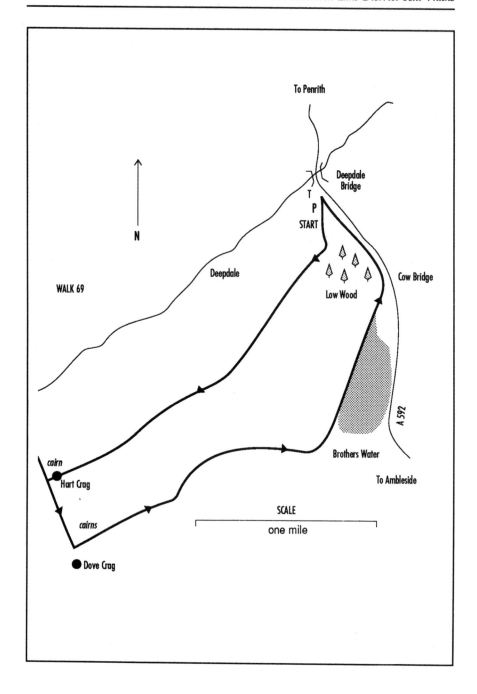

69. Hart Crag

This is an energy-sapping climb to the top of Hart Crag (2671ft/822m), along a three-mile long path from Deepdale Bridge. Return is down a track which starts at cairns a few hundred yards from Hart along the Dove Crag path. It is the fell path route mentioned in the last ramble and can be used in reverse instead of going over Stangs and Stand Crags in that walk.

Walking distance: 6.5ml/11.2km

Amount of climbing: 2177ft/670m

How to get there:

By car: Use Deepdale Bridge lay-by near telephone Box (MR399143).

Refreshments: See Walk 67.

Nearest tourist information: See Walk 65.

Ten yards from the telephone box in the Ambleside direction, follow a footpath sign. Just short of a barn, let the black and white arrow lead you over a ladder stile.

Through woods, the way swings right up the side of a wall. Over the next ladder stile spanning a wall, Gill Crag is left as you continue along a route mapped as Hartsop above How. Ignore the next ladder stile and continue on the straight-forward path over crags before the really exhausting part, a climb of more than 1000 feet to the top of Hart Crag, the ultimate summit on this route.

There is a cairn on top, where you have a choice of right or left. Your way is left along the Fairfield-Dove Crag path a few yards in front of the cairn. It is only a few hundred yards before you must look carefully for cairns leading off left. This is the path that leads on a downward spiral on scree that must be carefully tackled. On a flat bit, round a small tarn and later pass through a gate to emerge at the choice of ways sign for Dovedale: footpath or fell path. You have come off the fell path. A left turn takes you past a farm and Dovedale Cottage.

This track was used in Walk 68 from Cow Bridge car park. On this walk, however, continue beyond Cow Bridge on the Patterdale sign. This pleasant path between Low Wood and the main road has you at Deepdale Bridge car lay-by in about 10 minutes. Allow five hours, which includes a well-earned rest on Hart Crag.

Haweswater, with Hare Shaw coming in from the right

70. Hare Shaw

Hare where? That was the question asked by a regular Lake District walker when I disclosed the destination of my latest ramble. Hare Shaw is so remotely off the beaten track that the fell sheep appear to look on with shock when any other creature arrives on the scene.

Walking distance: 4.7ml/8km

Amount of climbing: 721ft/222m

How to get there:

By car: Park about $2^1/_2$ miles along the Mardale road from the start of Haweswater just short of a rocky bend where the first path starts. There is a lay-by in the rocks (MR479118).

Refreshments: See Walk 53.

Nearest tourist information: See Walk 53.

Proceed towards the head of the lake to a small gate and a signed Old Corpse Road Swindale public footpath. This is your way as described in Walk 64 as far as about a mile. Here, after a winding, tough climb, the path starts to drop towards Swindale Head.

Just before the drop look for a left-hand sheep track, opposite where the summer time field pattern in 1993 resembled an athletics track. Follow the track on a bearing of 300 degrees north west until you reach the summit of Hare Shaw (1638ft/591m), remembering you have started from 903ft/278m above sea level

The summit has a cairn distinguished from others nearby by a pole sticking out of the top. At the foot of Hare Shaw a well-defined cart track carries on over the smaller Powley's Hills and Long Rigg, to Harper Hills (1365ft/420m), which overlook a small reservoir.

From the cairn here, a track running left on 227 degrees south west follows a wall before leaving it to pass through a couple of gates and bend round faintly left with a glimpse of Haweswater, down right.

After a two-mile trudge from the reservoir, arrive back on the Old Corpse Road, where a right turn retraces steps to the car. Allow at least three hours.

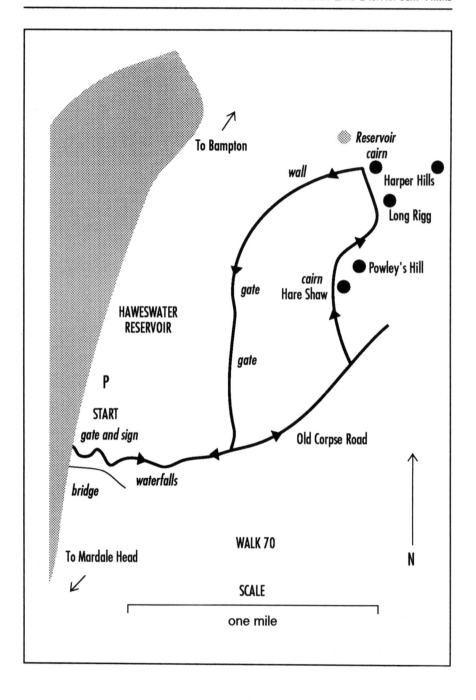

To Bampton

wall

Reservoir
cairn

Harper Hills

Long Rigg

Powley's Hill

gate

cairn
Hare Shaw

HAWESWATER
RESERVOIR

gate

P

START

gate and sign

Old Corpse Road

bridge

waterfalls

WALK 70

N

To Mardale Head

SCALE

one mile

71. Swindale Common

Weather can be treacherous on the open fells as photographer Bill and I experienced on this tramp over peat bog, tufty moorland and rocky outcrop in July. Gale force wind and rain lashed in our faces as we trudged over hills all under 2000 feet, yet challenging in the conditions.

Walking distance: 11ml/18.2km

Amount of climbing: 1462ft/450m

How to get there:

By car: See Walk 70.

Refreshments: See Walk 53.

Nearest tourist information: See Walk 53.

The first stage of the walk as far as footpaths are concerned is, on leaving the car, according to Walk 64 – the full two miles to Swindale Head along the Old Corpse Road.

At Swindale Head, reach the wooden signpost by the farm wall and turn through a gate (the opposite way to the finger pointing to Mosedale). Along the lane just short of another farm, follow a right-hand footpath sign near a footbridge, although the path crosses Mosedale Beck by means of stepping stones.

The way starts to rise here up the fell side, zig-zagging to a wall and continuing on 120 degrees south east, changing to 110 degrees after a cairn before crossing Goose Crag to a junction of ways and ford at White Crag.

A right turn here takes you over Gambling Moss and Hallmoss Hill to skirt Seat Robert (1673ft/515m) standing to the right. From that point, a walk of just under two miles brings you to a footbridge over Mosedale Beck, where the way is left for about half a mile to link with the Mosedale-Swindale Head track.

A right turn here starts you on a two-mile trek to Swindale Head, over the minor peaks of Ash Knott, Nabs Crag and Dodd Bottom.

Opposite the familiar wooden signpost at Swindale Head, the way is left, and left again near the post bearing waymarkers. From here the Old Corpse Road is retraced to the car.

Allow between six and seven hours for this one; it's rather tough!

Swindale Head

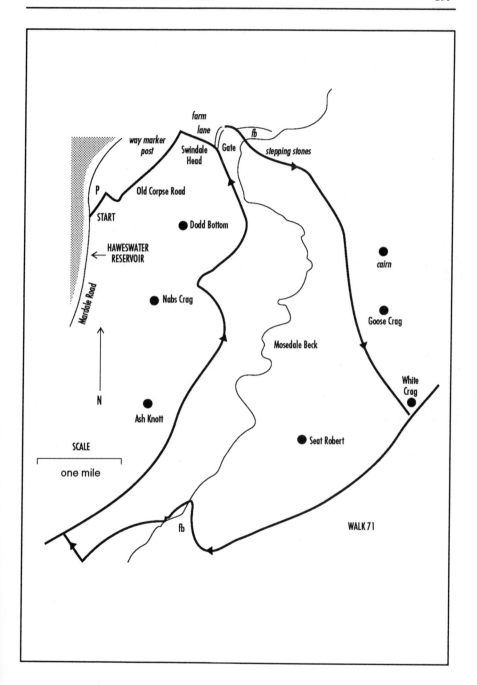

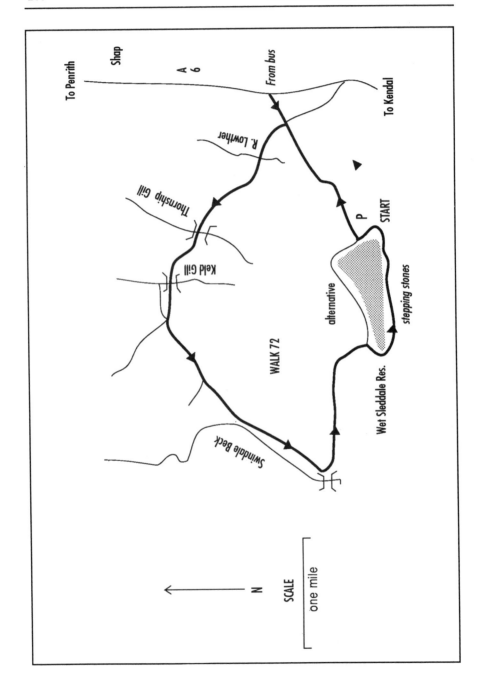

72. Lanshaw Hill and Dog Hill

Wet Sleddale Reservoir, Shap, where this tough to moderate walk starts and finishes, lived up to its name the day Bill and I ventured forth. It rained so hard the book containing my notes was sopping wet through and the writing indiscernible. To make matters worse, a stepping stone was missing over the beck on the last leg.

Walking distance: 8ml/14km

Amount of climbing: 260ft/80m

How to get there:

By bus: Penrith-Shap-Kendal.

By car: Wet Sleddale Reservoir car park (MR553117), approached along a lane signposted to Wet Sleddale on the A6 road south of Shap village.

Refreshments: Shap (Bulls Head, Crown Inn, Greyhound Hotel and Kings Arms for bar meals; café, shop and take-away for sandwiches, tea, coffee, burgers and pies).

Nearest tourist information: Penrith (see Walk 53).

Although the amount of climbing seems modest, you start from a high base of 877ft/270m above sea level and the going, for the most part, is tough.

From the car park retrace steps along the lane by which you travelled over two cattle grids and go left at the cross tracks, passing Kemp Howe on the right. If a bus traveller, ask for the nearest stop to Wet Sleddale lane and walk down a lane to the same cross-tracks, which are only a short distance from the main road. Turn right here.

Past Kemp Howe, cross the River Lowther, Thornship Gill and Keld Gill to reach cross-roads. Go left on the lane with "30" and "sheep" signs. This track climbs round over Lanshaw Hill (910ft/280m) and Dog Hill (1066ft/328m), the latter looming up in front just after a left fork takes you away from Tailbert Head which is to the right, at the front of a copse.

A bearing of 245 degrees takes you on a way running above and parallel with Swindale Beck. Soon the path runs down to the beck at a cattle bridge, where you embark on a cart track climbing left over Gouther Crag and Glede Howe with Great Ladstones to the left.

The way now becomes slightly complicated as it tends to stray from the mapped path, but keeps roughly on the same bearing until the reservoir can be seen again. Here, zig-zag right near old farm buildings to cross stepping stones, where one was missing over Sleddale Beck.

If the stone is still missing and you don't fancy the adventure, go back up the hilly field and follow the track near a sign at one of the farm buildings which keeps above the other side of the reservoir. Then cross the embankment to the car park or continue along the lane to the road for the bus.

If you have succeeded in crossing the beck, go left alongside the reservoir to come out by the car park at a wooden footpath sign.

Allow about six hours.

Wet Sleddale and Lanshaw Hill

73. Sleddale Pike

The sight of three deer strolling over the top of Sleddale Pike was a bonus on this trudge over mostly wet ground and grouse shooting land, which must be avoided once the season starts on August 12th.

Walking distance: 4.5ml/8km

Amount of climbing: 1350ft/450m

How to get there: See Walk 72.

Refreshments: See Walk 72.

Nearest tourist information: See Walk 72.

At Wet Sleddale Reservoir car park, follow a brown wooden bridleway sign on 220 degrees south west over a ladder stile; then, go left at a fork towards a building where you pass through two gates within a few yards.

On 180 degrees south start heading over the moor towards the unmistakeable mast on the big hill. Over a home-made beck bridge and through the right-hand of two gates across a cart track, pass grouse butts on the right.

Eventually a grassy path climbs towards the mast, swinging right to keep line with a wire fence. Where you can look down left towards old buildings go right on 30 degrees north west, finding a sheep track taking you to a cairn on top of Sleddale Pike. Fork left to a broad peaty track and turn up left to another cairn. Where Wet Sleddale Reservoir comes into view, swing right and go right to the next cairn and head towards a large boulder seen in the distance, on 30 degrees north east. Pass more shooting butts and head for a track you can see and go left across a stream towards an egg-shell blue building, which is the lunch house for the game hunters. From the lunch house a green track continues over a beck bridge, over another beck and through a gate.

The broad track meanders on towards the trees. Where the track bends right, follow a fence and jump a ditch near a large drain pipe, heading towards the industrial towers of Shap. Through the right-hand of two gates near a babbling brook with a rustic fence crossing it, go through another gate on the track back to the car.

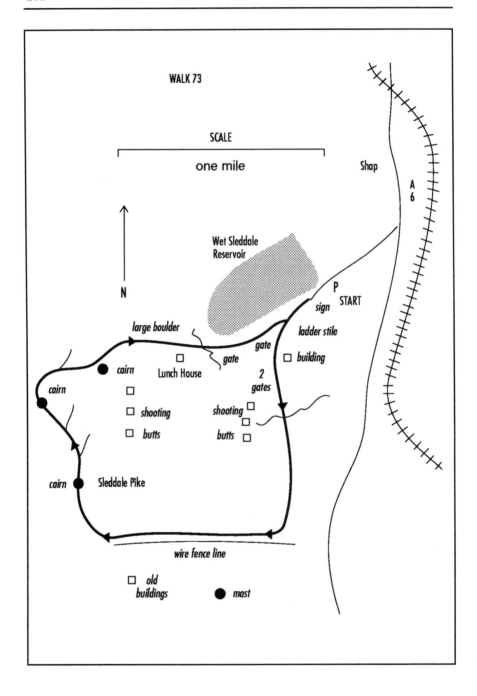

WALK 73

SCALE

one mile

Shap

A
6

Wet Sleddale
Reservoir

N

P START

sign

large boulder

ladder stile

gate

gate

building

cairn

cairn

Lunch House

2
gates

shooting

butts

shooting

butts

cairn

Sleddale Pike

wire fence line

old
buildings

mast

74. Outscar

This is the first of two family walks with little height to finish the section. A plus point is the number of wild flowers. Spoiler, however, was that Bill and I had to survive two bull fields. But the bulls were with dairy cows; so have faith in the Wildlife and Countryside Act!

Walking distance: 3.2ml/5.3km

Amount of climbing: 227ft/70m

How to get there:

By car: A6 lay-by (MR550189) on right a couple of hundred yards under M6 motorway bridge travelling from Penrith.

By bus: Penrith-Kendal (CMS).

Refreshments: See Walk 72.

Nearest tourist information: See Walk 72.

From lay-by, walk a few yards towards Shap village on the same side of the road. Follow a bridleway signed to Scarside. Through a gate, go diagonally right through the next gate and left through a further gate. Diagonally right across this field, pass through a small gate and across the next field towards young trees. Go through another little gate and continue through a plantation.

Yet another gate leads into an open field which you cross ahead, through another gate and between woods to reach a broad metalled track. Turn right on 110 degrees south east, crossing a cattle grid after about 200 yards and another one into a farm complex.

Opposite a tyre dump, take a metalled road between meadows. Go through an agricultural compound via gates. Diagonally right near a wood, enter the right hand of two gates into a field and keep the wood on the left before going through a five-barred gate.

Keep a castle-like stone structure on the right and then left through a gate. Another gate takes you straight ahead through a field and the two small gates you used on the outward journey. Now reverse part of the outward route to return to the lay-by.

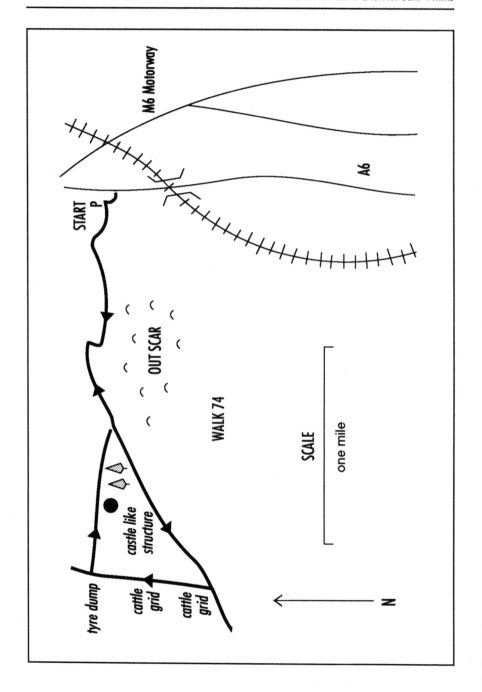

Who says the best thistles are in Scotland? Outscar takes some beating.

75. Bartigills Crags

Although most of the crags are overgrown with grass, there is sufficient height to give a good bird's eye view of part of Ullswater. There is also the chance to see Dacre Castle and Church.

Walking distance: 4ml/6.7km

Amount of climbing: 240ft/74m

How to get there:

By car: From Penrith along A66 towards Keswick. Turn left at roundabout along the A592 (Ullswater road). First right, next left, over cross roads into a cul-de-sac road. Park in a convenient spot at the bottom of a road near a public footpath sign (MR484276).

Refreshments: Stainton (Kings Arms and Brantwood Hotel)

Nearest tourist information: See Walk 72.

As well as taking in the edge of Bartigills Crags, the route goes over Lough Hill (540ft/180m). It is a pleasant stroll compared to the usual hill walk standards, starting from a path to the right of the cul-de-sac end.

The Dacre footpath sign is on the other side of the cul-de-sac end. Broad to start, the path narrows between hedgerows at a broad track coming in right. Entering the Lake District National Park, go over a wooden step stile and follow a way marker to the right.

A buzzard flew across our path as Bill and I climbed a ladder stile in the left-hand wall to stroll through part of Evening Bank Wood.

A latch gate in the field gives access to rising land, with Ullswater views. Over gate and stile with way-marker, head across field through wall gap and traverse another field towards a further wood, ignoring the left-hand gate.

Through a gate ahead, bend right, then left through another gate on a 250 degrees bearing, over the next field, through a gate, straight ahead and open another gate with a farm on right.

Turn left here through a small gate at the side of a big one. Up field for a few yards, swing right, go diagonally left and round to left of a wall.

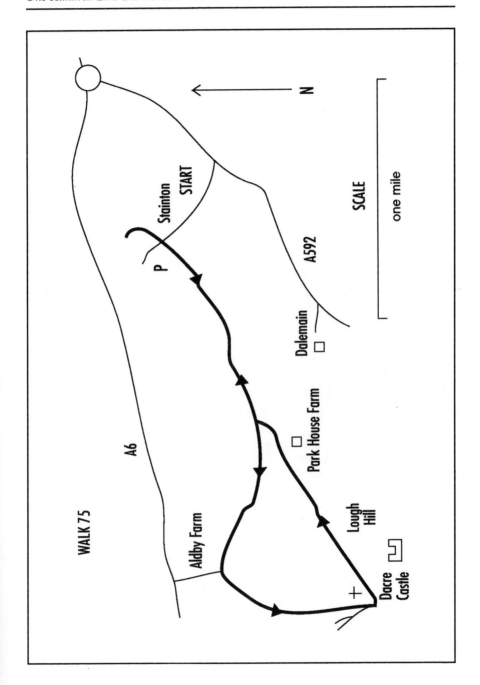

WALK 75

A6

Aldby Farm

Stainton
START

P

A592

Dalemain

Park House Farm

Lough
Hill

Dacre
Castle

N

SCALE

one mile

Through a gate, enter a copse along a cow path for a couple of hundred yards and cross a right-hand stile with the hedge on the left.

Pass through a small gate and repeat the exercise a few hundred yards on to walk diagonally right to go through another small National Park gate and then through an iron one.

Through two way-marked gates, pass a cottage and the Church of St Andrew in Dacre. Follow the lane to the T-junction. Turn left to view Dacre Castle, dating from the early 14th century and with the ghosts of three ancient kings reputedly in the grounds.

Retrace steps a few yards to a metal gate on the same side of the road. Pass through the gate and keep the church on the left. Over a ladder stile, pass over Lough Hill. Bear left to a wall and pass over another ladder stile with a way marker.

Then a fence stile is surmounted, a field crossed over another ladder stile near a farm building, and slightly right and over a stile at the side of a left-hand gate.

At "No right of way" gate, turn left and quickly right and left again, skirting Park House farm. Through a gate, turn right, over a ladder stile and keep by the right hedge. Pass a right-hand gate, but go over a stile at the next gate and head on slightly diagonally right. Uphill over part of Bartigills Crags again, pass over a wooden step-stile at the side of a gate.

Straight ahead through woods and across a field, pass through a wooden gate taken on the outward journey. The path goes through a wood over a wall ladder stile and then upfield between stone walls. Over another stile at a gate side, turn left and follow another woodland path into a broad track between stone walls to return to your car.

While in the area, visit Dalemain, with Norman pele tower, off the A592 towards Ullswater. There is an admission charge.

The South East

These walks are covered by the South East Sheet of the English Lakes Outdoor Leisure series.

76. Red Screes

Red Screes dominates Kirkstone Pass, but the usual way to tackle it is from Ambleside.

Walking distance: 9ml/14.48km

Amount of climbing: 2400ft/426m

How to get there:

By car: Parking in Ambleside (MR378045).

By bus: Keswick-Lancaster service.

By Lake Windermere steamer: From Windermere.

By train: Windermere, then steamer or bus.

Refreshments: Ambleside.

Nearest tourist information: Old Courthouse, Church Street, Ambleside. Telephone (05394) 32582.

The first stage is on the road up the pass. Leave Ambleside by turning left off the Keswick road past the Golden Rule pub (MR377047). There is nothing complex or exciting about the direct route up the ridge.

At first, the path is not particularly well marked when you leave the Kirkstone pass road at the second footpath sign. It's boggy and the walking is sometimes soggy.

One plus mark is that you are between two walls which point the way upward to your destination. The summit of 2540ft is a welcome sight. Red Screes gets its name from the ruddy coloured stones that can be spied from miles away.

The crags and scree that frown down on Kirkstone make up for the dull approach work from Ambleside. It is possible too, to go up from Patterdale, but this means a long road trek.

Scramble down to the pass to make a quick three-mile descent down the road. Some sections are steep. Kirkstone was not known as *The Struggle* for nothing in the days when carriage passengers had to get out and walk.

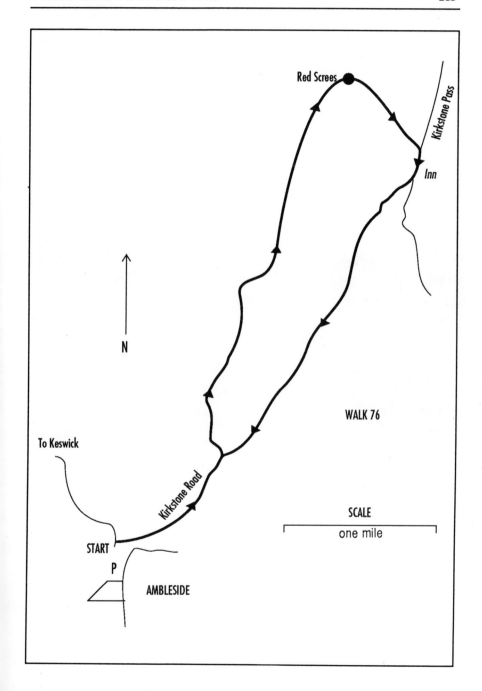

Red Screes

Kirkstone Pass

Inn

N

WALK 76

To Keswick

Kirkstone Road

SCALE
one mile

START
P
AMBLESIDE

Another way up from Ambleside involves crossing Sweden Bridge and going up Scandale Pass. Scandale is the only link with another mountain, Little Hart Crag, just half a mile away.

Whatever the route, Red Screes has one main asset. Views of the High Street range are superb.

Red Screes from Brotherswater

77. Heron Pike and Nab Scar

Really part of the famous Fairfield horseshoe. Heron Pike tops 2000ft but the real star is Nab Scar, the first summit on the way up. Nab Scar is a steep, craggy terrier of a fell above Rydal.

Walking distance: 6ml/10.14km

Amount of climbing: 1600ft/487m

How to get there:

By car: Park on the private road off the A591 road at the side of Rydal Church (MR365062). From Keswick direction it is on left at a large sign to Rydal Mount, the poet William Wordsworth's home for many years. However, avoid parking in front of the cottages.

By bus: Keswick-Lancaster service (CMS).

Refreshments: Rydal Hall.

Nearest tourist information: See Walk 52.

Along the private road, Rydal Mount stands to the left. But instead follow a concrete ramp. Go right through an open gate then left past buildings in a yard. Another gate with an erosion control sign leads to the fell path.

Follow the pitched, man-made, stone track, spiralling up the fell. Climb a wall stile and continue up the erosion control path. It is twisting and steep in places. As height is gained and the fell opens out, look back for a superb view of Windermere; Rydal Water shimmers below and there is a glimpse of Grasmere beyond. A rough track leads to another wall stile and on past the indeterminate summit of Nab Scar, usually taken as a large cairn back from the edge of the cliffs, near a crumbling wall.

A simple path on grass trails on to Heron Pike (1852ft/570m) less than a mile away. Where it splits either track can be taken. A quartz outcrop marks the summit, which is anything but a pike.

The best views to be had on this walk are of the Coniston and Langdale fells. The descent retracing the steps to Rydal is as easy as the ascent is tough. *Warning:* In misty conditions, do not be tempted to take any other path than the one to Rydal.

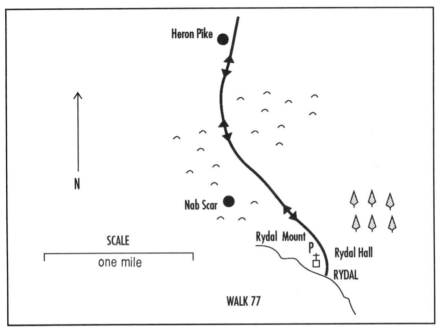

Grasmere and Rydal Water from Heron Pike

78. Wansfell

A climb that often causes confusion because Wansfell and Wansfell Pike are not the same. The pike is slightly lower than the 1547ft top of the fell.

Walking distance: 6ml/10.14km

Amount of climbing: 1500ft/457m

How to get there:

By car: Park in Ambleside (MR376039).

By bus: Keswick-Lancaster service (CMS). National Express coaches stop and pick up in Ambleside.

Refreshments: Ambleside.

Nearest tourist information: See Walk 38.

Leave the town from behind the Old Salvation Inn. Head for the Stock Ghyll waterfalls, one of which thunders 60ft into the ravine. Another possible route out of the town is by Blue Mill Road and the gasworks. This is not recommended. The objective, Wansfell Pike, is visible all the way from Stock Ghyll.

A clear path, steep in later stages, is easily followed. The rocky summit of the pike provides a fine view of Windermere. The actual summit of Wansfell is a grassy hump, usually marked by a few stones. Unlike its neighbour, no fine views are on offer.

Descent can be varied from Wansfell Pike to the 17th century village of Troutbeck. A path drops down, via gate and stile to Nanny Lane and on to the village. A path, Robin Lane, leaves the road near the post office. But a short detour can be made to Town End, a 17th century house owned by the National Trust.

Back on Robin Lane follow the path over a bridge and on the High Skelghyll and Skelghyll wood. This leads to Ambleside town centre by way of the old lake road. This is a climb for clear days. Paths up are obvious enough, but the tops are confusing.

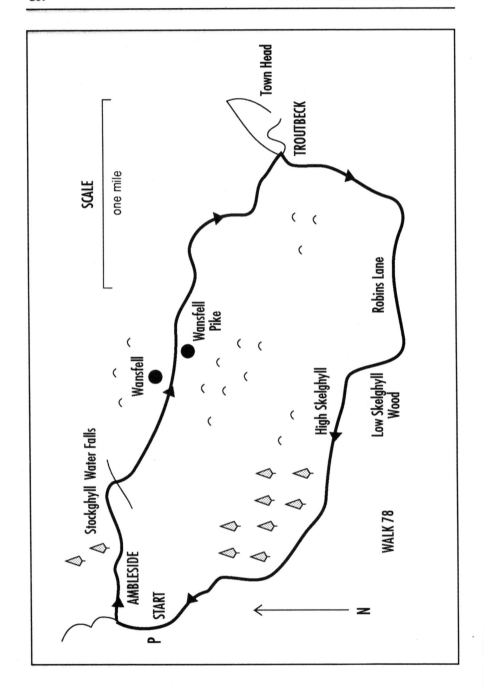

SCALE

one mile

Town Head

TROUTBECK

Robins Lane

Wansfell
Pike

Wansfell

Low Skelghyll
Wood

High Skelghyll

Stockghyll Water Falls

AMBLESIDE

P START

WALK 78

N

79. Kentmere Pike and Harter Fell

Kentmere is off the beaten track from Staveley between Windermere and Kendal. A fine horseshoe walk is the reward for venturing along the leafy lanes to Kentmere village.

Walking distance: 9.5ml/16.3km

Amount of climbing: 2200ft/679.2m

How to get there:

By car: Parking is available, with luck, at the village church (MR456041).

Refreshments: Tea and cake at the farm near Kentmere Church; tuck items at Kentmere Post Office; Staveley; Windermere.

Nearest tourist information: Victoria Street, Windermere. Telephone Windermere (05394) 46499.

Follow the road, High Lane, for a mile or so to Hallow Bank. A gate to the right of a sprawl of buildings leads to the open fell.

The path leads up a groove to a wall. A series of zig-zags follows, with the trail not always obvious, and it then moves through another wall gap and on to the grassy upper slopes. An ordnance survey point marks the summit of Kentmere Pike standing just under 2400ft/738m.

From here, a relatively uninspiring stroll can be turned into something special by tackling the ridge route to Harter Fell, just over a mile away to the north. Walls and old broken fence lines serve as markers. Harter Fell at 2534ft/780m is more imposing than its neighbour, with its summit cairns decorated with a weird array of ironmongery from broken fences.

The next stage is to pick out the track to the west and Naw Beild Pass, a superb crossroad. Care is needed here in mist.

Walk a few yards from the summit cairn on the pass to view Small Water, Haweswater and the lofty heights of Riggindale. The track back to Kentmere, steep initially, passes Smallthwaite Knott and leaps back to Hallow Bank Quarter. Becks are forded at a couple of points to reach the grassy lane to Kentmere village. It is worth noting that the return route can be varied to visit Kentmere reservoir.

Kentmere Pike is on the extreme left

In poor conditions this walk is best contracted to an ascent on Naw Bield Pass. Views from Kentmere Pike are restricted, possibly the best being across Windermere to Morecambe Bay.

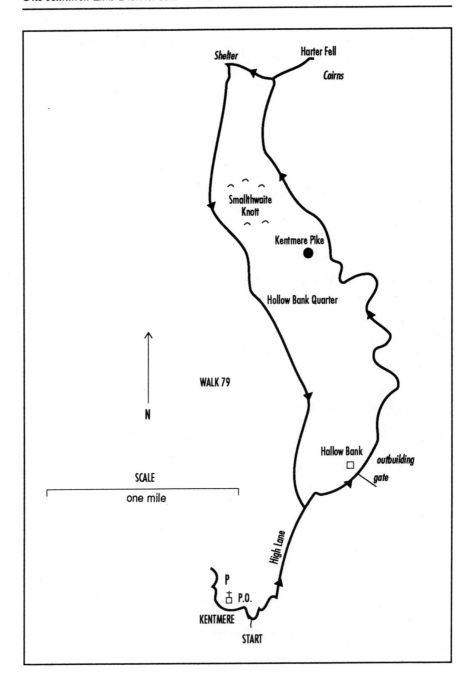

80. Lingmoor Fell

Fell adventure finishing with a delightful stroll alongside Great Langdale Beck, this is a walk for the hardy rambler.

Walking distance: 4.2ml/7km

Amount of climbing: 1110ft/370m

How to get there:

By car: Park at Elterwater. Choice of three car parks. Walk starts from the one with a telephone box near Great Langdale Beck (MR328047).

By bus: Ambleside-Dungeon Ghyll 516 service (CMS).

Refreshments: Hotels and shop, Elterwater.

Nearest tourist information: Redbank Road, Grasmere. Telephone (05394) 35245.

Out of the car park over the beck road bridge, follow the left-hand bend past the youth hostel and take the first turn right. Climb, and just past Elterwater Hall, on the left go right along a lane marked cul-de-sac.

Straight up the metal road, through Sawrey's Wood, look for double domestic chimneys peeping through the trees on the right and take the bridleway on the opposite side of the road, through stone pillars. Keep on the main track and ignore left-hand shoot-offs. Arrive at an open space and old slate quarry with Chapel Stile and church in the Langdale valley to the right. Continue round the left-hand edge of the slate pile and over a step stile.

The grassy way winds left at a "no path" sign. Take the right fork a few yards up, surmount another step stile into a field and follow a path alongside the right-hand stone wall.

At a point where you may look back at Windermere, the path winds right at a cairn to pass a "danger" notice.

Use the path ahead to reach Lingmoor Fell summit (1407ft/469m). Pass a stile on the right. Use winding paths to keep the wall on the right and follow cairns over the crags on 280 degrees to reach the craggy top via a right-hand step stile in the fence.

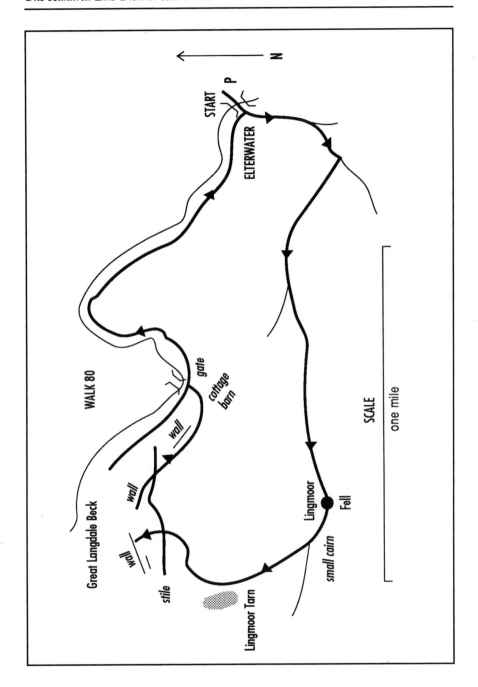

Due north from the summit, look down on the oddly shaped Lingmoor Tarn, towards which you head and take a right-hand path with a small cairn at the head.

Down to the tarn, keep it on the left over a wet, undulating path to start the way-finding adventure. Drop right on 40 degrees north east with the Dungeon Ghyll hotels over and down to the left.

Drop further to cross a beck near a small waterfall and climb through the heather, which is a delightful purple and as good as the Scottish variety in mid-summer.

Follow the path round to re-cross the beck and embark on a tricky way to reach a wall. Climb here to a step-stile where a view may be had of Blea Tarn and the Side Gates Road. This is not your way and you must now back track on the path without crossing the stile.

The well-worn path gradually wends away from the route you took to reach the stile, but crosses it. The path winds over a beck as you follow it through the growth by the left-hand wall.

After much perseverance, find a T-junction with a small gate to the left. Go right over a beck, still following a left-hand wall through a small wicket gate at the side of a large gate.

Climb slightly to follow one way-marker after another to the left of a barn before turning left at a cottage. You can say you have gone down to safety as you follow a broad track and keep the Great Langdale Beck bridge on the left to pass through a gate.

The elevated path alongside the beck is a nice walk over a stile and wire instead of the cattle grid. Over a stile near the camp site, keep an old bridge on the left and continue through woods and over a stile and bridged beck with a disused quarry on the right.

Ford two becks by stepping stones. Keep alongside Great Langdale Beck on the same side, following the right-hand bend, away from a wooden footbridge, continue along a lane. At the junction, cross the road bridge to the car park.

81. Holme Fell

The start from the often-bypassed Yew Tree Tarn on the A593 Ambleside-Coniston road gives Dad a chance to have a walk while the rest of the family feed the ducks. Once ascended, Holme Fell (1030ft/317m) affords a fine view of Coniston Water.

Walking distance: 2ml/3.7km

Amount of climbing: 682ft/210m

How to get there:

By car: Lay-by alongside Yew Tree Tarn on the A593 road for parking (MR321002).

Refreshments: Coniston (2ml).

Nearest tourist information: 16 Yewdale Road, Coniston. Telephone (05394) 41533.

Towards Coniston the path skirts the tarn over a footbridge through Harry Guards Wood and passes over several becks before taking you over a stile.

Through a left-hand wall gap, follow boggy ground and then a wire fence to the left to pass through another wall gap accompanied by a gap in the netting to embark on a well-trodden path through ferns. At a narrow, stony track go right and climb to a point where Yew Tree Tarn and your car can be seen looking back.

Four cairns are passed on an undulating trip to a choice of three ways. Select the left one to the big cairn, the summit of Holme Fell, a mixture of rock and grass. A disused reservoir can be seen below with a smaller one peeping through the trees in the background.

This is where Coniston Water is seen to all its glory 200 degrees south west and is your direction, through heather, fern, grass and bog and over rock. Gain a little more height with Coniston still visible and drop down a gully and crags, some covered in moss.

A passage through trees takes you to a path running parallel with a stone wall. Descend right on this stony path through ferns and turn right alongside a wall on your side of a gate. Under Calf Crag, meet another path at a wall corner and turn left to surmount a step stile to a lane, where the way is again left.

Just before the beck bridge, go through a left-hand gate on the Skelwith Bridge marked path, over a ladder stile by a gate and along a track to the A595 at Yew Tree Farm.

Bear left for the couple of hundred yards of main road walking to return to the car lay-by.

Swans on Yew Tree Tarn overlooked by Holme Fell

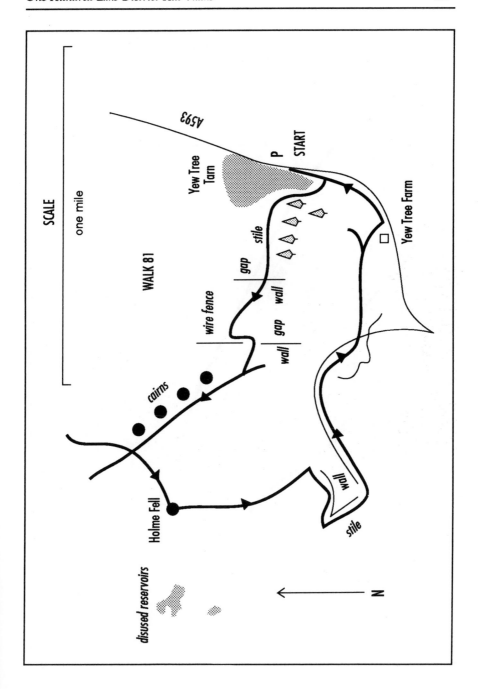

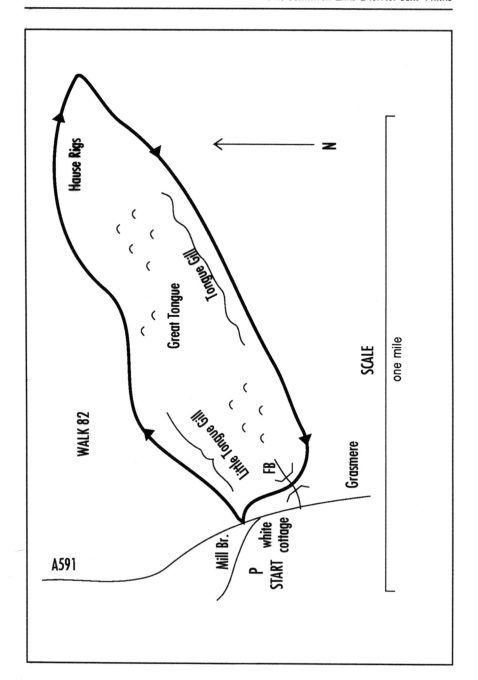

82. The Tongues

A rocky round taking in Great Tongue, Little Tongue and Tongue Gill where mountain mist can descend suddenly.

Walking distance: 3ml/5km

Amount of climbing: 1784ft/549m

How to get there:

By bus: Keswick-Kendal (CMS and National Bus) to Mill Bridge.

By car: Park at Mill Bridge on A591 on space at the corner of a lane opposite a white cottage (MR339098).

Refreshments: Grasmere.

Nearest tourist information: Grasmere. See Walk 80.

Take the Patterdale bridleway at the side of the white cottage and pass through a gate near further cottages and continue up the left-hand side of Little Tongue Gill, skirting the Great Tongue massif.

Ignore a wall gap, before going through a small gate near a waterfall and either fording or bridging a beck to continue climbing roughly left. Cross another ford as the path bends left. It is a winding path that keeps going on 74 degrees north east.

Where you reach rough land at Hause Riggs, where there is no path on the ground in front of you is where you start the homeward journey on a path that doubles back right on 99 degrees south west. Eventually you hit a broad, green path leading down.

It is a descent all the way now on the same compass bearing as paths run into paths down the side of Tongue Gill. Drop to cross a footbridge near a reservoir and rejoin the outward track in reverse, back to the car.

Allow about two hours.

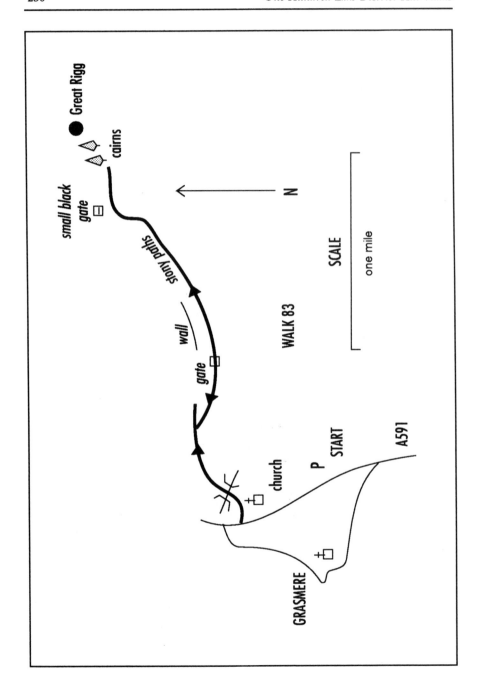

83. Great Rigg (from Grasmere)

Mist can also be a problem on this out-and-back walk giving the Grasmere approach to Great Rigg, a peak also covered in the North East section from Dunmail Raise.

Walking distance: 2ml/3.2km

Amount of climbing: 2275ft/700m

How to get there:

By bus: Keswick-Kendal (CMS and National Bus) to Our Lady of the Wayside Roman Catholic Church.

By car: Park in lay-by on A591 between the two Grasmere village lanes (MR341075). Opposite Grasmere Sports Field.

Refreshments: Grasmere.

Nearest tourist information: Grasmere. See Walk 80.

Walk towards Keswick and turn right along a lane at the side of Our Lady of the Wayside Roman Catholic Church. The lane bends left over a bridge to a junction, where the way is right. After a few yards take a right-hand footpath signed to Greenhead Gill.

Through a gate on a stony path, find another stony way left and follow an arrow, swinging right at a small black gate. Follow the cairns as the path gains height and eventually reaches the summit of Great Rigg.

Doing an about turn back to the car, you soon find there is more than one route down. I followed a white arrow, then a yellow one near a wall, not far from where I was able to look down on Alcock Tarn.

Keep dropping through the ferns and you cannot go wrong heading for the buildings of Grasmere in the distance ahead. A lane is reached and at the Greenhead Gill sign we followed on the outward journey turn left and left again at the next junction and repeat the exercise at the church on the main road to return to the car lay-by.

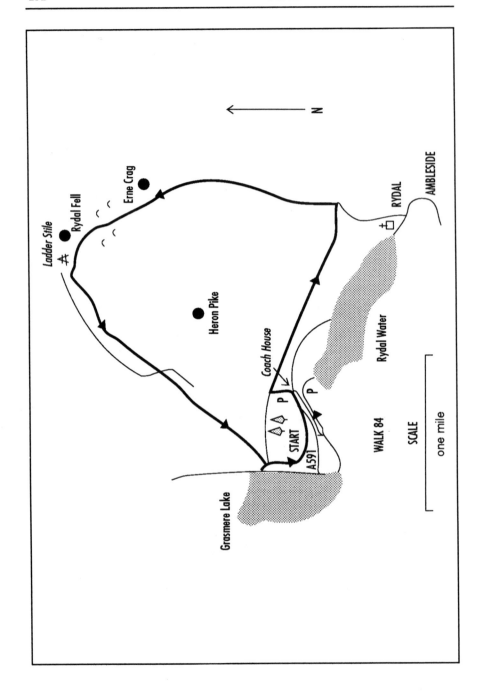

84. Rydal Fell

Rydal Fell comprises several peaks, including Nab Scar, Lord Crag, Heron Pike and Erne Cragg. This walk starts over Nab Scar to Rydal and then climbs alongside Rydal Beck to Erne Crag and the summit of Rydal Fell (1998ft/615m). The return is on the Heron Pike side down to the main road near Rydal Water.

Walking distance: 6ml/10km

Amount of climbing: 1800ft/600m

How to get there:

By bus: Service 555 Keswick-Kendal (CMS) and National Bus.

By car: Choice of two pay car parks either side of A591 near Rydal Water. White Moss Common (MR347064).

Refreshments: Rydal Hall (see OS map, MR365063).

Nearest tourist information: Grasmere. See Walk 80.

From the car park on the opposite side of the main road to Rydal Water, follow a footpath at the side of Coach House and take a right turn through the left-hand of two gates to a T-junction, where the way is right through small gates.

At a way-marked T-junction, go left on the footpath sign and follow the sign through a farmyard and through a wicket gate at the side of a big gate, on the way to Erne Crag and Rydal Fell summit. Over a ladder stile, turn left and follow the path as it drops through ferns and eventually follows the left-hand side of a beck.

Cross the beck and descend through more ferns to a Brackenfell notice. Turn left through a gate to a lane, which you follow to the Rydal lane sign, where you go left for about 300 yards to pass through a black iron gate on the right and eventually down stone steps through woods to reach the main road, near Bannerigg guest house, opposite Grasmere Lake.

Go to the left and cross the road to take the embankment path through more forestry to the end of the lake. Parallel with the road, pass through a gate alongside an attractive beck. Through two further gates do not cross a quaint footbridge, turning left from it towards the road. Over a small beck bridge, fork right near toilets and go left at the junction with the main path and left again to one of the car parks.

Rydal Caves on the banks of Rydal Water are worth a detour. The caves were man-made by slate quarrying.

85. Scandale and High and Low Pikes

The vicinity of Scandale Fell, Scandale Head, Scandale Pass and High and Low Pikes can hog low cloud. There had been plenty of rain when I did this walk in August 1993. As a result, the peaty and boggy surface was turned into a mud-bath.

Walking distance: 7.5ml/12km

Amount of climbing: 2112ft/650m

How to get there:

By bus: Keswick-Kendal (CMS and National Bus) to Ambleside.

By car: Car parks in Ambleside. Most convenient behind Bridge House (MR375046).

Refreshments: Ambleside (numerous).

Nearest tourist information: Ambleside. See Walk 76.

At the western end of Ambleside town, the "Kirkstone 3" road sign is unmistakeable. Walk along this for about 10 yards before turning left and continue along Nook Lane, through Nook End Farmyard and wind past woods along a broad cart track onto open fell. The upward path is clear until you get branches when it is necessary to keep on a 360 degrees north bearing.

Keep climbing over Low Pike and High Pike (2132ft/656m) until you reach the third cairn. Here, near a wall which I found to be a sheltered lunch stop and, at roughly a three-mile mark, turn right on 110 degrees south east.

After about a mile during which you will pass an unusual group of cairns to the left, cross a ladder stile in a right-hand wall and embark on the Scandale Pass.

This is an attractive walk back into Ambleside on the way to where you may find a photographic proposition in High Sweden Bridge, an attractive Lakeland stone packhorse bridge down to the right. Do not cross it for the walk. Your path keeps straight on. It eventually becomes a lane. Head back into town by a choice of more than one permutation.

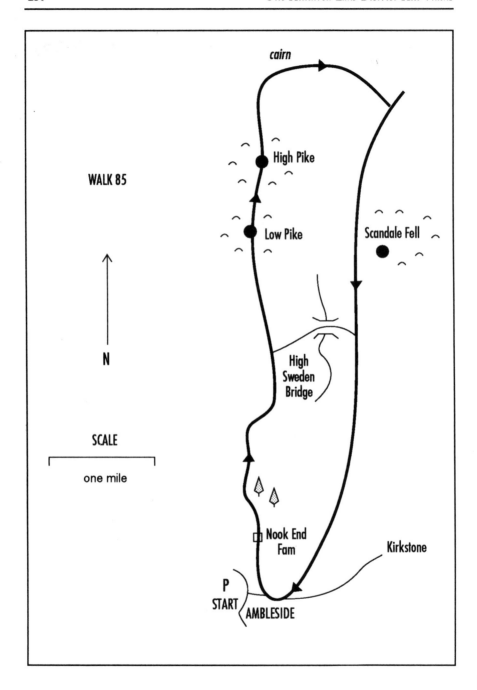

WALK 85

cairn

High Pike

Low Pike

Scandale Fell

N

High
Sweden
Bridge

SCALE

one mile

Nook End
Fam

Kirkstone

P
START
AMBLESIDE

86. Tom Heights and Tarn Hows

Tarn Hows, a peaceful stretch of water lying between Ambleside and Coniston, is probably more well known to Lake District visitors than the summit on this walk. The two combined make a rewarding hour and a half walk on land owned by the National Trust, who have constructed access for the disabled round the tarn, which they bought from Beatrix Potter more than 60 years ago.

Walking distance: 2ml/3.2km

Amount of climbing: 390ft/120m

How to get there:

By car: Tom Gill National Trust car park, on the A593 road at Yewdale Beck Bridge (MR314997).

Refreshments: Coniston.

Nearest tourist information: Coniston. See Walk 81.

In the car park, keep a Tom Gill National Trust sign on the right as you pass over a footbridge spanning Yewdale Beck and taking you through the delightful Tarn Hows Wood.

With the beck on the right, take a left fork. The way swings left on what becomes a broad track with a picturesque waterfall on the right. At cross paths go left and climb, following footpath sign on right.

Through a small gate, you soon arrive at Tarn Hows water, a place to stop and admire. Turn right on the lakeside path through another gate and straight on, ignoring the path left.

Just short of a passing place sign, go left. Follow the path running parallel with the tarmac overlooking the tarn. After a few yards go through a National Trust gate and up right on grass.

On higher ground, turn left on a narrow path to the stone on top of a crag inscribed to the memory of Sir James and Lady Anne Scott, of Yews, 1930.

Go left along the main track at what appears to be a milk stand. Keep on the high path and swing left at a farm building known as Rose Castle.

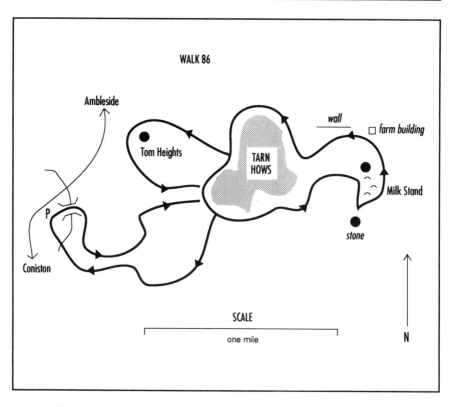

Now follow the path nearest to the lake and from a wall end drop onto the tarnside path and turn right.

Through a gate, go right to sweep over Tom Heights (874ft/269m) and go right once the main path is rejoined.

Beyond another gate, take the extreme right-hand grassy uphill track which forks right after a few yards. At the next track, drop right and sharp right at a ruin. Straight ahead over a beck, a gate puts you on a stony track with a right turn for the car park.

87. Park Fell

Park Fell (812ft/250m) affords remarkable views of the Langdales and Elterwater. The walk takes less than an hour.

Walking distance: 1.7ml/2.5km

Amount of climbing: 325ft/100m

How to get there :

By car: Lay-by near entrance to Park Farm, wooden shelter and post box, on A593 Coniston-Ambleside road (on the left from Coniston). MR334028.

Refreshments: Skelwith Bridge (hotel and tea garden).

Nearest tourist information: Ambleside. See Walk 76.

Opposite the wooden shelter, which is towards Skelwith Bridge from the lay-by, follow a bridleway sign at the side of Park Fell House. In about 200 yards follow a faint left-hand path up the hillside.

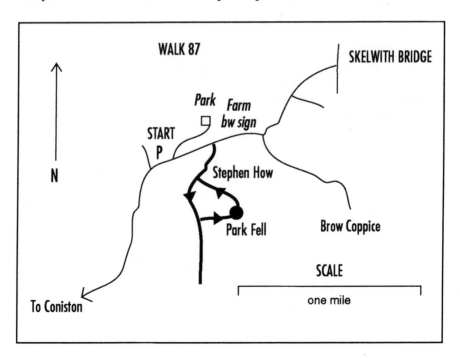

The path winds to a wall-end. Follow a beck and climb as high as you can. This is the summit of Park Fell. Enjoy the views of the Langdales and Elterwater and move on a compass reading of 340 degrees north. Drop down left to follow the beck and reach the wall again.

Descend to the main track and turn right back to the main road bridleway sign and a left turn to the car or a wait for the bus.

Looking to Park Fell from Tilberthwaite

88. Buckbarrow Crag

Buckbarrow Crag is one of the many fine peaks surrounding the infrequently visited gem of Long Sleddale. The route starts and finishes at a pretty packhorse bridge in as peaceful a spot as anyone could imagine.

Walking distance: 2.6ml/4.2km

Amount of climbing: 325ft/100m

How to get there:

By car: About six miles down the Long Sleddale lane off the Kendal-Penrith A6 road. Park at Sadgill Bridge (MR482057), less than two miles beyond car park at church, old school, telephone box and toilets.

Refreshments: Stockdale Craft Shop (tea and coffee), between church complex and Sadgill Bridge.

Nearest tourist information: Town Hall, Highgate, Kendal. Telephone (0539) 725758.

From Sadgill packhorse stone bridge, spanning the River Sprint and near a farm where there is a mountain rescue kit, take the stony track which does not cross the bridge and continue with the bridge and farm to the left.

After about a mile near where waterfalls come into view, take a right-hand ladder stile over the stone boundary wall. The path goes left and gradually swings up the hillside over one lot of crags and over onto Buckbarrow Crag (1625ft/500m), at the back of which is wire fencing.

Keep it on the left as you go over undulating ground. The fencing encloses this "fold" and descends right over tricky crags and grass that is slippy after rain.

Take great care down this sheer drop as boundary wall replaces fencing and leads you to a gate on the main track, where a left turn and about a quarter of an hour's walking gets you back to the car.

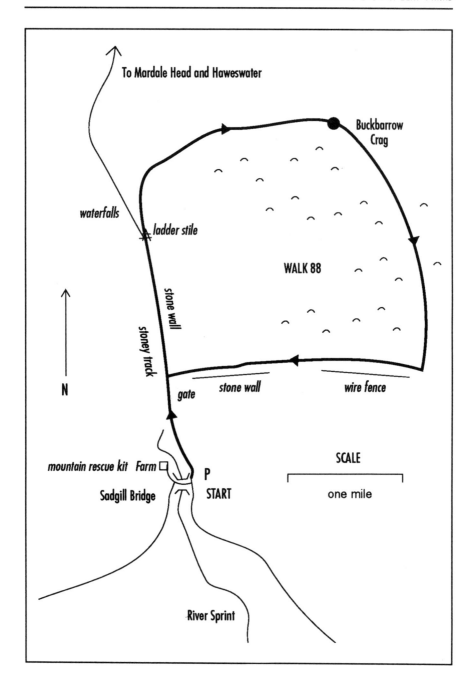

To Mardale Head and Haweswater

Buckbarrow
Crag

waterfalls

ladder stile

stone wall

stoney track

WALK 88

N

gate

stone wall

wire fence

SCALE

mountain rescue kit   Farm

P
START

Sadgill Bridge

one mile

River Sprint

89. Green Quarter

This is another light and delightful fell walk from Sadgill Bridge in Long Sleddale, this time touching on Kentmere.

Walking distance: 5.4ml/9.7km

Amount of climbing: 767ft/236m

How to get there:

By car: Park at Sadgill Bridge, but be sure not to obstruct (MR483057). See Walk 88 for directions.

Refreshments: See Walk 88.

Nearest tourist information: See Walk 88.

In contrast to Walk 88, this time you cross the lovely Sadgill Bridge and, walking away from the farm, go through an iron gate on a path swinging right at a farm building.

Marked as a byway to Kentmere, the stony track passes through two further iron gates to follow the High Lane, Kentmere, sign at a junction of paths straight ahead.

With a beck on the left, pass a cairn and climb over a ladder stile before forking left through a wooden gate just before farm buildings. At the end of the byway turn left on a lane through a wall gap. This is the hamlet of Green Quarter. After about 100 yards take a left-hand track and cross a meadow diagonally right.

Pass through the highest of two gates and follow a broad, grassy track up a walled field. Keep left on entering a wood with Kentmere Church down far right and squeeze between a wall and a tree. Climb to a track, go left and at the second fork take the narrower and fainter of the two tracks.

Continue on this path and take your pick between a gate and a ladder stile. Over a beck, head for another ladder stile with the rock of Green Quarter summit (1381ft/425m), to the right.

Over another ladder stile at the side of a gate, pass cairns and arrive at the gate and High Lane sign, from where you may retrace steps to the car.

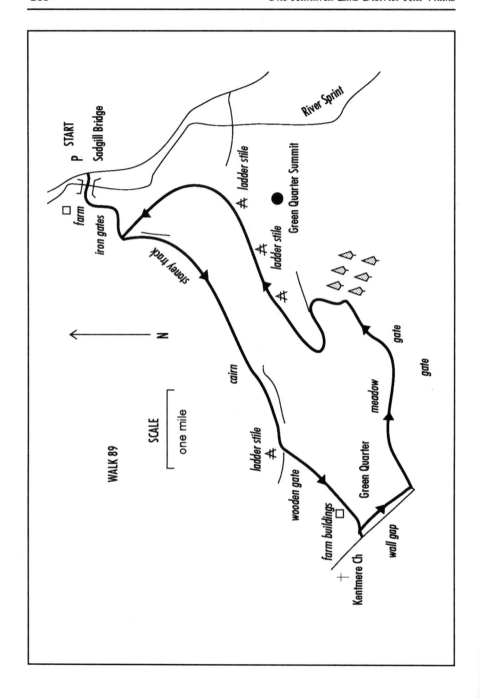

90. The fells around Skeggles Water

The fells around Skeggles Water take in Cocklaw Fell and some boggy ground where avoidance will only be achieved by self-initiative.

Walking distance: 5ml/8km

Amount of climbing: 357ft/110m

How to get there:

By car: See Walk 88.

Refreshments: See Walk 88.

Nearest tourist information: See Walk 88.

The first part is as for Walk 89 until you reach the High Lane, Kentmere, sign, where a deviation is made left. Pass a ladder stile in the left-hand wall and go over a beck through a gate with a broken wall on the left. Dip over a beck and climb diagonally right.

Through a gate, continue on a compass bearing of 250 degrees south west, swinging left at the unmistakeable highest point in the vicinity, Cocklaw Fell. With Skeggles Water in view to the left, do not be tempted to head for it, as the ground is swampy.

Continue to a junction of paths with the comparative giant of Staveley Head Fell ahead and turn left. Do a far skirting of Skeggles Water on a left-hand turn and soon, on higher ground, you will spot a wood down to the right.

Keep this on the right as you drop towards the River Sprint to find a wire fence with a wooden fence for crossing at the far right-hand end. Turn left past a ruin and a white farm cottage and go over a bridge to the road.

Left on the road, Stockdale Craft Centre and Workshop for tea and coffee is down the right-hand lane, but continue for Sadgill Bridge.

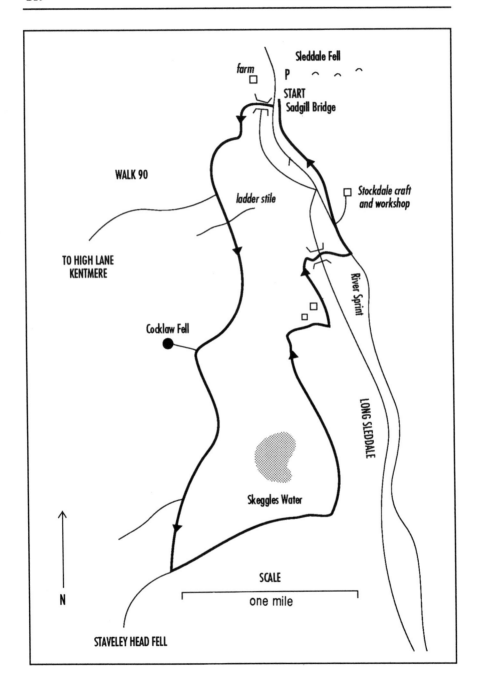

91. Hugill Fell

This a short walk with a rewarding view from the top of Hugill Fell, one of the lower range on the Park's eastern fringe.

Walking distance: 2.7ml/4.7km

Amount of climbing: 175ft/54m

How to get there:

By car: Park on grass at Browfoot (MR455007).

By train: Windermere-Oxenholme BR line to Staveley. Out of station, follow lane straight ahead through the village and across the old main road for just under two miles to Browfoot Farm.

By bus: 555 service Keswick-Kendal (CMS) to Staveley.

Refreshments: Staveley (shop, pub, etc).

Nearest tourist information: Windermere. See Walk 79. Kendal. See Walk 88.

Where the lane from Staveley, meandering by the River Kent for a while, bends sharp left at Browfoot, Browfoot Farm is to the right and your start to the left and a left-hand footpath sign a couple of hundred yards along the lane.

Through a gate, climb the fell side and follow the grassy path to a gate in a wall gap and climb round the high crag on the left to a gap in the wall near a line of trees.

Here you start the climb to the top of Hugill Fell, its pillar monument being unmistakeable. Before you reach it, however, you are confronted with a stone wall. Go right here to get through a gap stile in the wall's lower corner.

Diagonally left uphill to the pillar, you will find a plaque dedicated to the memory of Thomas Williamson, of Height in Hugill, Gent, who died February 13, 1797, aged 66. Erected 1803.

Leave the pillar on 150 degrees south east towards a gate and wall to take a left turn on a track.

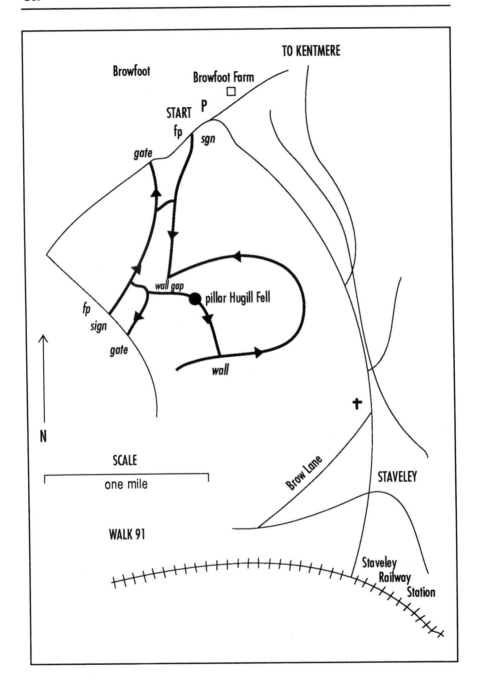

TO KENTMERE

Browfoot   Browfoot Farm

START   P
fp   sgn

gate

wall gap

pillar Hugill Fell

fp
sign

gate

wall

N

SCALE

one mile

Brow Lane   STAVELEY

WALK 91

Staveley
Railway
Station

Through a wall gap, reach a right-hand wall with another gap. Do not go through this, but follow a narrow path left to go through the next gap. Wind left through a further gap and round the fellside with the pillar now up left. From the wall gap stile you came through on the upward journey, aim for a gate down right leading to a broad track.

Turn right and after a few yards take the footpath sign over a step stile. Diagonally left over the rocks, go over an old gate filling in a wall gap. The same direction takes you to a gate and the lane where you are either parked to the right or follow back to Staveley.

The summit of Hugill Fell with memorial cairn

92. Wansfell and The Hundreds

Wansfell is more well-known as a name to Lake District wanderers than The Hundreds. But Wansfell and its sister Wansfell Pike are part of The Hundreds along with White Crag and Chimney Crag. It can be misty up there, as Bill and I found in mid-August.

Walking distance: 3.5ml/5km

Amount of climbing: 1163ft/484m

How to get there:

By car: Park in space just past Troutbeck Church and nursery school on left towards Kirkstone on the A592 road (MR413028).

Refreshments: Limefitt Caravan Park (see Walk 93).

Nearest tourist information: Windermere. See Walk 79.

To start a nice "pull" in pleasant surroundings, walk back a few yards to a bridleway starting between a VR 1887 drinking fountain and the church. Along the bridleway to a big grey gate, follow the opposite yellow arrow over a stile.

Through swing gates above a tributary of Trout Beck and another gate where the beck goes away from the path, turn left at cross roads for about 100 yards before taking a right-hand bridleway.

At the end of the stony track, go left on the lane for a couple of yards to follow the Wansfell sign at the side of Lanefoot Farm. Through a small gate at the side of a big one, continue up this stony track to cross a wooden step stile at the side of a gate and go through iron double-gates, one like a kissing-gate.

Through a proper kissing-gate now and over a wooden footbridge and several minor becks, you eventually get reward for the foot-slogging by reaching a cairn on top of Wansfell Pike (1573ft/484m).

The way down from the top starts at a right-hand stone wall, which you keep on the left along a path which is not quickly seen at first, but is just short of a ladder stile.

Keep descending on the path to eventually pick up the outward route in reverse.

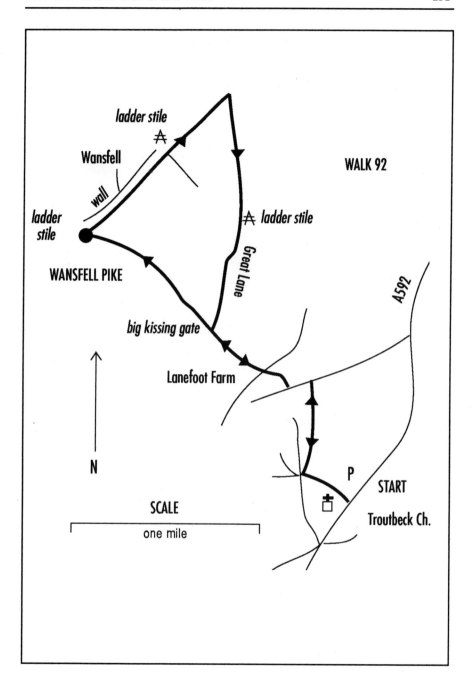

ladder stile

Wansfell

wall

ladder stile

WANSFELL PIKE

ladder stile

Great Lane

WALK 92

A592

big kissing gate

Lanefoot Farm

N

SCALE

one mile

P

START

Troutbeck Ch.

Kirkstone Pass old coaching inn, 1500ft above sea level, is along the Pass towards Patterdale: an additional nearby place for refreshment $3^1/_2$ miles from Troutbeck Church.

93. Park Fell Head, Threshthwaite Mouth, Thornthwaite Crag and High Street

Quite a trudge for a few miles, before gaining height to reach Threshthwaite Mouth and a right turn for the beacon on Thornthwaite Crag. A trek over part of High Street before dropping back to Troutbeck.

Walking distance: 9ml/14.7km

Amount of climbing: 2275ft/700m

How to get there:

By car: Park as for Walk 92.

Refreshments: Limefitt Caravan Park (Haybarn Inn, Ramblers' Bistro and take-away Spar shop).

Nearest tourist information: See Walk 79.

Towards Kirkstone, find the entrance road into Limefitt Caravan Park. Follow the winding road and the footpath signs and those for the refreshment spots. Just beyond the Ramblers' Bistro and Take-away Spar shop, go left on a bridleway sign, at a white house. This bridleway is also a favourite with pony trekkers.

Through double iron gates, follow the left-hand stone wall through Long Green Head farmyard. At the far end keep on the main track and over a concrete beck bridge and a couple of fords to maintain a direction over the lower slopes of Park Fell Head along a grassy track to reach a broad track where the way is right and through another gate.

The main beck is on the right as you head for the confluence of hills which is Threshthwaite Head. On arriving at a stone wall, the left turn is for Stony Cove Pike, but our way climbs right to the significant chimney-like cairn of Thornthwaite Crag, from where a 150 degrees south east bearing takes you to cross paths. A right turn on 210 degrees south west leads along High Street and a quickly descending path with Hagg Gill on the left. At the foot, keep direction and pass an entrance to Long Green Head before crossing Ing Bridge over Trout Beck.

Shortly, a signed footpath left leads you across a field by-passing Town

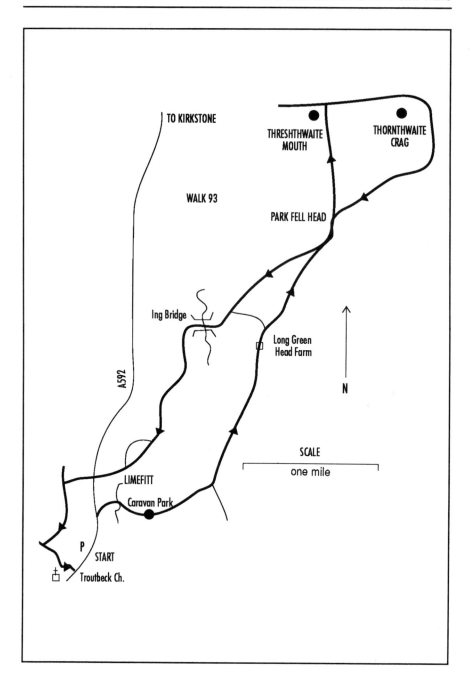

TO KIRKSTONE

THRESHTHWAITE
MOUTH

THORNTHWAITE
CRAG

WALK 93

PARK FELL HEAD

Ing Bridge

Long Green
Head Farm

N

A592

SCALE
one mile

LIMEFITT
Caravan Park

P
START
Troutbeck Ch.

Head and down a lane left to the main Kirkstone road. Cross into a lane and at four-pronged sign post familiar from Walk 92, go left and left again at the grey gate to skirt Troutbeck Church yard and go short left on the main road to the car.

The purpose behind crossing the main road into the lane and taking the footpaths is to avoid some potentially unpleasant road walking.

Windermere from School Knott (see Walk 94)

94. School Knott

Planners who allowed a housing estate to be established in the shadow of School Knott spoiled a splendid holiday walk in Windermere. The stroll starts promisingly until the Oxenholme-Windermere railway is crossed. Then one has to navigate one's way through a jungle of modern dwellings before finding the way to continue. Once reached, School Knott provides rewarding views.

Walking distance: 4ml/7.4km

Amount of climbing: 279ft/7.4km

How to get there:

By car: Most convenient car park is Broad Street, near council offices, signposted to the left along the main street from Windermere railway station (MR413985).

By train: Windermere is the terminus for the Lakes line from the main West Coast line at Oxenholme.

By bus: Windermere is served by the Lancaster – Kendal – Ambleside – Keswick 555, sometimes referred to as Keswick – Kendal.

Refreshments: Windermere (numerous).

Nearest tourist information: Windermere. See Walk 79.

With the good sense of direction that walkers usually have, those of you travelling by car can pick a way through the streets to the railway station, from where the route can conveniently start for motorists, train and bus passengers alike.

On the main road above the station, walk in the Kendal direction until passing Thwaites Lane and Orrest Head Farm on the right. Follow a wooden footpath director hidden by chevron signs and go through a wall gap and a small wooden gate, straight ahead over a field with the farm on the right.

Through a big gate with kissing gate, aim for School Knott, the big hill ahead, and then fork through an iron kissing gate in the right-hand corner.

Descend stone steps. Keep to the right and cross a wooden step stile in

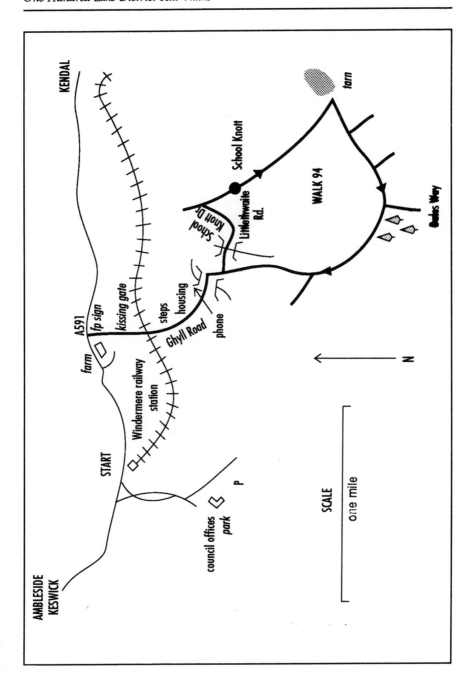

the hedge. Follow the path left over the railway, down steps and over a ladder stile.

Now starts the tour through the housing estate. Straight on down Ghyll Road, bend left at the phone box. Turn right at the "no tipping" sign and left on Linethwaite Road over a bridge. Left again and up School Knott Drive, there is a hard-to-find "footpath to School Knott" sign integrated with street signs, on a wall.

Back in the country, turn right on cross-paths and go through a kissing gate at the side of a big gate and follow the footpath diagonally left, climbing to a further kissing gate. Follow the path up over a mound to School Knott summit, a splendid view point for Windermere and the Langdales beyond.

At the extreme foot from the way you ascended is a delightful little tarn on compass bearing 120 degrees south east. Down to the tarn, go right through a kissing gate and ignore two stiles on the left. Keep along a broad track and turn right at a Dales Way sign junction by a wood.

Through a big gate, fork right on the main, low track, through a gate, straight on down a lane, passing a Lickbarrow footpath sign. Through another gate, towards a white house on a hard path, reach a T-junction and turn left over a bridge.

Now it is housing estate revisited time. With Mill Rise and Brow to the right, go right on the next road and through a garage site before crossing the railway on familiar ground. It should be easy now with the aid of the sketch map, to retrace steps back to Windermere station.

An average time would be two hours.

95. Scout Scar

Scout Scar is a massive escarpment and a focal point around Kendal with a dramatic western side drop to farmland. This route follows the limestone outcrops in a horseshoe.

Walking distance: 4ml/7.4km

Amount of climbing: 55ft/17m

How to get there:

By car: Parking space in cleared quarry area opposite entrance to Scout Scar on the Underbarrow road between Bowness-on-Windermere and Kendal, off the B5284 at Crook (MR488924).

Refreshments: Underbarrow (inn).

Nearest tourist information: Kendal. See Walk 88.

It seems unbelievable that you climb only 55 feet on this exhilarating walk. The reason is that most of the climbing has been done before the start – by car! You start from a base of 692ft/213m and the summit is 747ft/230m above sea level.

The starting path is diagonally right across the road from the car park entrance. Through an iron kissing gate there are three ways. Take the right-hand stony track, meeting a seat along on the left to the memory of Edward Johnson, Tynemouth and Windermere.

Keep left at a fork to reach a shelter and view point for the Kent Estuary and surrounding fells. Continuing along the main track there is a dramatic drop right towards Barrowfield Farm and fields. Go left on the next broad track.

At a four-path meeting, keep central to the stone wall and turn left. Harebells and heather are an autumn feature on this plateau. Follow the path which keeps the wall to the right and left on a broad track running parallel with the bottom wall, the perimeter of a road.

Slightly climbing, keep left for a few hundred yards to cross roads and a wall gap right. Pass near a cairn where a rocky outcrop comes into view and keep in line with the right-hand wall.

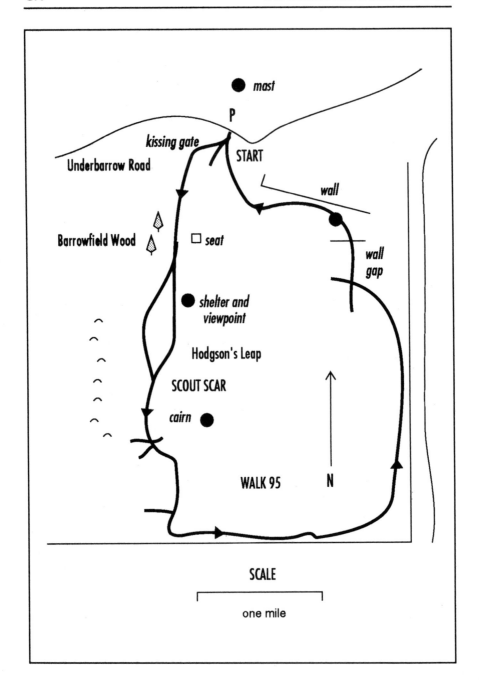

mast

P

START

kissing gate

Underbarrow Road

wall

Barrowfield Wood

seat

wall gap

shelter and viewpoint

Hodgson's Leap

SCOUT SCAR

cairn

WALK 95

N

SCALE

one mile

This path eventually veers away from the wall. Keep direction on a broader track, slightly climbing again, but again nothing in terms of feet.

The track continues ahead at a wall corner and through a kissing gate. Turn right on a north bearing alongside a white stone wall, heading for the mast in the distance.

You emerge at the iron kissing gate used on the outward journey, but by what was then the left hand of the three tracks. Over the road, go diagonally right to the car park.

Allow between two and three hours.

Morecambe Bay from Scout Scar

96. Whitbarrow Scar and Lord's Seat

Another scar, but certainly not a scar on the landscape. This is a beautiful walk through a nature reserve with almost a guarantee of spotting a red deer or two.

Walking distance: 9.5m/16km

Amount of climbing: 682ft/210m

How to get there:

By car: Lay-by with telephone near Gilpin Bridge Hotel. Turn in from A590 to A507. A few yards on left near Lake District National Park boundary sign (MR469855).

Refreshments: Gilpin Bridge Hotel.

Nearest tourist information: Victoria Hall, Main Street, Grange-over-Sands. Summer only. Telephone (05395) 34026.

This start is almost level with the sea, so the amount of climbing is more distinctive. Walk towards Windermere and take the first track left to Gilpin Farm House, where a left turn with a tributary of the River Gilpin left takes you to the edge of the A590 road. The lane right keeps you off the road and takes you along a right-hand drive to Raven's Lodge, opposite which follow a bridleway sign with a blue and yellow arrow.

Through a gate between trees, behind dwellings, go ahead on track and almost level with left-hand gate posts go up right through woods to wind right on a broader path. Right at the next junction was where Bill and I spotted our first deer of the walk.

Up left at a seat, follow a 350 degrees north west bearing through a wall gap at a junction. Pass a cairn on a view point, with a brilliant view of the Kent Estuary. Follow a series of cairns over Whitbarrow Scar and then a stony path in the same direction towards Lord's Seat (698ft/215m) with a pinnacle, passing through a wall gap into the Hervey Natural Reservoir. There are two cairns on either side of the path.

The pinnacle reached is dedicated to the founder of the Lake District Naturalists' Trust, Canon G.A.K. Hervey, 1893-1967, after whom the reserve, managed by Cumbria Wildlife Trust, is named.

Continue for a few yards but swing down right gradually to a right-

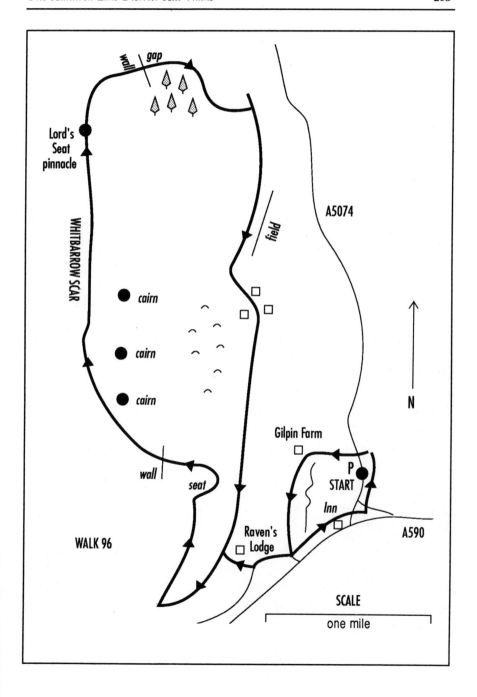

wall gap

Lord's
Seat
pinnacle

WHITBARROW SCAR

A5074

field

cairn

cairn

cairn

Gilpin Farm

P
START

Inn

wall

seat

WALK 96

Raven's
Lodge

A590

SCALE

one mile

N

hand wall gap stile. From here, ignoring a left turn, follow a clear path through the forestry. Turn right at a T-junction on 150 degrees south east bearing. Further on in the trees, another deer was seen and the deer soon saw us! Left on a broad track and straight ahead where another route comes in right, pass a right turn but go down right where another path comes in left.

Ignore another right turn and stick to the main track before turning next right, where a green field can be seen over the perimeter wall of the wood. Follow the narrow, winding path down to a house and round right to pass between buildings.

Straight ahead on the track with Levens Church in the distance left and the Scar up right, emerge at a footpath sign on the lane near Raven's Lodge, familiar from the outward journey. Now, keep on along the lane, over a cattle grid this time to go left along the main road verge, following the Cumbria Cycle Way sign over a bridge.

Left on the Bowness-in-Windermere A5074 sign, pass the Gilpin Bridge Inn (if not going in!) and go left before the next bridge back to the lay-by.

Whitbarrow Scar rises above the forest track

97. Furness Fells

The east side of Coniston Water is not frequented as much by walkers as the opposite bank, which boasts Coniston Old Man. Nevertheless, several fine walks can be had on the Furness Fells with good views of Old Man and the water.

Walking distance: 4ml/7.4km

Amount of climbing: 1092ft/333m

How to get there:

By car: Off the A5084 road at Lowick Bridge, turn immediately left over River Crake. Through High Nibthwaite for three-quarters of a mile, find a space in trees bearing sign "next car park 1 mile". (MR298909).

Refreshments: Lowick Green (Farmers' Arms).

Nearest tourist information: Coronation Hall, County Square, Ulverston. Telephone (0229) 57120.

From the car park, follow a track going away from the "lake" into the trees. Climb through the forest and then descend. Straight on and round a fallen tree, take the higher fork of two and go over a right-hand fence stile to turn left on a broad, stony track with a beck on the right.

There is a waterfall on the right as the way bends left, on the side of which Coniston Old Man and Dow Crag come into view. After an undulating stride-out, Coniston Water can be seen almost along its full length. As the stony track starts to dip, take the uphill track over Great Hill (1092ft/333m) and after a few yards fork left through the ferns. Soon, as the path swings round, Morecambe Bay will be ahead in the distance. Surrounded by rocks, the track veers right towards a large outcrop. Veer round alongside a right-hand wall and through a gap stile with a way-marker. Straight ahead towards a tree-covered house, keep it to the left and pass over slates bridging a beck. Turn left and go down a track, pass a ladder stile, but surmount the next one to turn right on the Parkamoor path sign. Reach a broad, green track with a stile and gate to the right. Turn away from it and carry on with Coniston Old Man over left on a due north bearing.

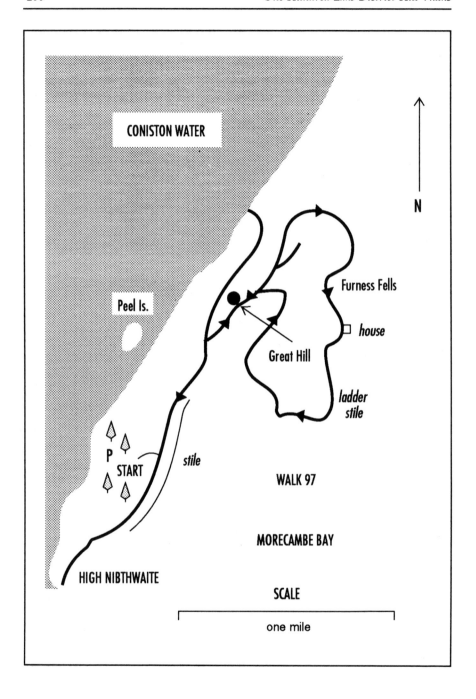

CONISTON WATER

Peel Is.

Furness Fells

house

Great Hill

ladder
stile

N

P

START

stile

WALK 97

MORECAMBE BAY

HIGH NIBTHWAITE

SCALE

one mile

You now find yourself on the same track you were on before. Heading towards Old Man, the "lake" is soon seen down left. As the path rises you are level with the island on Coniston. The path emerges on the broad stony track of the outward trek. Turn left and back over the high fence stile on the right, through the woods to the car.

Coniston Water, looking across to Coniston Old Man from the Furness Fells

98. Latterbarrow

Hawkshead seems to be crying out for a footpath map on distribution at the tourist information office. A family wanting Latterbarrow, the high point overlooking Wordsworth's school-day village, could only get a street map. So they found the way by following Bill and me.

Walking distance: 3.2ml/5.3km

Amount of climbing: 577ft/176m

How to get there:

By bus: Coniston Rambler (CMS) Bowness-Ambleside-Hawkshead-Coniston.

By car: Car parks in Hawkshead village (MR354980).

Refreshments: Hawkshead (numerous).

Nearest tourist information: Main car park, Hawkshead. Telephone (05394) 36525.

From the main car park, walk towards the camp site at the T-junction and turn left. Where the road bends left, follow a footpath sign right. Over a bridge and through a gate, go diagonally left through a kissing gate and right.

Through another kissing gate, go left on the Loanthwaite arrow, over a stile with a dog lift and through a gap and gate stile. Diagonally left and through another kissing gate, go over a step stile to follow white-top posts.

The other side of yet another kissing gate, it is left again. Keep the farm left to pass through the next kissing gate and turn right on the lane. Left at the T-junction for about 20 yards, find the right-hand footpath sign, through a gate and up the stony track to the top of Latterbarrow.

On the way, you follow a left fork and turn right on grass to get to the tall cairn on the summit (803ft/245m). Facing Hawkshead village from the top, go left on the path down to a stile at a wall and follow the Hawkshead sign right. Arrive at the path junction of the outward trek and retrace steps to Hawkshead.

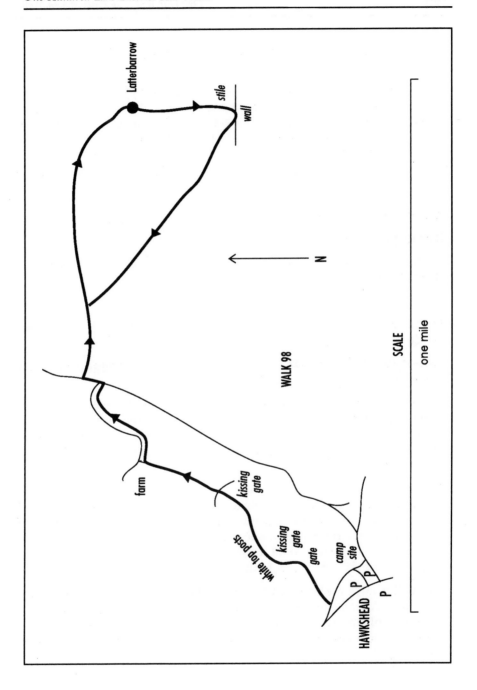

99. Black Combe

This is a rarity in the book which is better done by train than by car. The start and finish are between two railway stations on the Cumbria Coast Line. A car, however, may be left at one station, travelling by train to collect it. Whichever way you travel, the goal is Black Combe (1969ft/900m) and its little sister White Combe (1358ft/415m). The views are superb. No wonder poet William Wordsworth received inspiration up here while looking down on the Duddon.

Walking distance: 10ml/15km

Amount of climbing: 1875ft/574m

How to get there:

By train: BR Cumbria Coast Line (Barrow-Carlisle) to Silecroft. Return from Green Road.

By car: Parking space at both stations.

Refreshments: Silecroft (Miners Arms and Post Office/shop); The Green (Punch Bowl).

Nearest tourist information: Millom Folk Museum, St George's Road, near Market Square. Telephone (0229)772555.

Leaving Silecroft Station, the Miners Arms is on the right before you reach the A5093 road, crossed diagonally left into a footpath signed Black Combe. At the dwellings go left to cross the A595 into a stiled path which reaches a tarmaced track.

This becomes stony after the house and reaches a right-hand fork, along which pass through a gate bearing a notice about dogs. Now for a steady climb of about two-and-a-half miles before a plateau leads to the cliff edge. Here, veer right with a sheer drop on the left. The trig point for Black Combe summit is right as you continue for a few hundred yards before making for cart tracks to the left.

Follow this track for best part of a mile. The sea and Bootle village, come into view. After taking a right fork, come face to face with a gate at a T-junction of tracks. Turn right. The track eventually fizzles out as you cross the gorse and drop to where you can see a sandy track and gate across a beck.

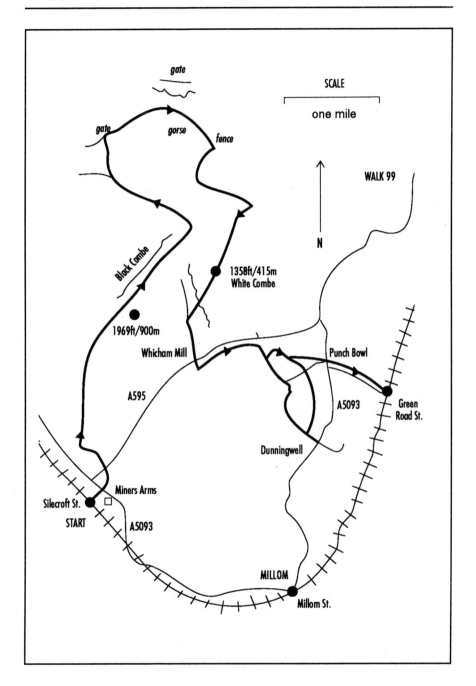

SCALE
one mile

N

WALK 99

gate

gate

gorse

fence

Black Combe

1358ft/415m
White Combe

1969ft/900m

Whicham Mill

Punch Bowl

A595

Green
Road St.

A5093

Dunningwell

Miners Arms

Silecroft St.

START

A5093

MILLOM

Millom St.

Do not go through the gate but go right, following the left-hand fence on another steady climb, that eventually goes from fence corner to fence corner and reaches White Combe summit. The main guide is the beck below, right, with which the path keeps in line for well over a mile.

Continue through the thick gorse. On spotting a broader track on the other side of the beck, there is more of it to drop through, as that track is now your aim. On reaching it, go left and continue down to a gate near Whicham Mill Cottage. This is an attractive tree-gladed spot, a place to linger. There are nice tree trunks on which to sit.

Off this quiet lane, there should be paths to the left providing a short cut to the main road. I failed to find them, so continued along the lane. Turn left on the A595 road for a kilometre and take the right-hand lane signed to Dunningwell. A hundred yards or so along this lane, follow a footpath sign on the left marked The Green.

This is easy to follow at first as it goes through kissing gates to cross the track to Brockwood Park. After a gate, go right to a stone squeezer stile (no-one over nine stone!). From then on, the path is hard to find. Do not take the clear one leading over the left-hand rise; your way is diagonally right across-field with woodland over to the right.

Passing through gates, you eventually reach a lane. A left turn takes you to the A5093, which has veered round in a semi-circle through Millom town since you left it at Silecroft. Cross the road into a lane at the side of the Punch Bowl and continue for three-quarters of a mile to Green Road Station.

100. Claife Heights

Nothing was more satisfying for Bill and me than to relax in the sunshine on top of Claife Heights. I looked over to Windermere and fells we had conquered and know that we were a short stroll away from finishing the last of these One Hundred Lake District Hill Walks

Walking distance: 3ml/4.7km

Amount of climbing: 550ft/253m

How to get there:

By car: You will find that the car parks immediately in Near Sawrey are taken up by visitors to Hill Top, the celebrated former home of Beatrix Potter, the children's writer. However, about 200 yards through the village towards Windermere, is a lay-by on the left (MR372355).

By bus: Coniston Rambler. See Walk 98. Alight Hill Top.

Refreshments: Near Sawrey (Tower Bank Arms, Buckle Yeat and cream teas in a courtyard on the opposite side of the road).

Nearest tourist information: Hawkshead. See Walk 98.

Diagonally left opposite the Tower Bank Arms, embark on a bridleway. At the junction for Far Sawrey and Claife Heights, take the latter. Ignore all shooting off tracks and keep on the main stony track.

Through a gate and over a ford, the delightful Moss Eccles Tarn is on the left of the bridleway. Fork left at a "private" sign and through another gate, reach the equally pleasant Wise Een Tarns.

Continue, but rather than go through the gate into the forestry, turn right with the wall and follow the path to the top of Scale Hill, the summit of Claife Heights (550ft/253m).

Soak up the view of Windermere over left as it seems to be slanting towards you. Keep it left as you swing down through a wall gap ahead and over boggy ground to the next summit with Wise Een Tarns now down to the right. Reach the track of the outward journey and retrace steps to Near Sawrey.

At the end of this, the hundredth walk, Bill and I toasted in Lucozade!

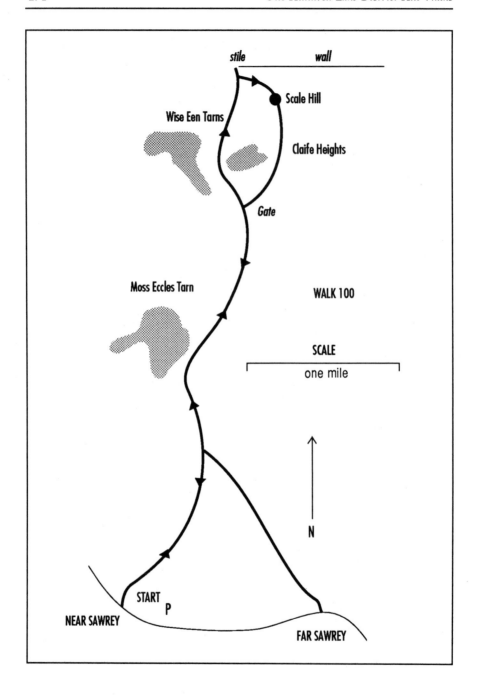

Explore the Lake District with Sigma!

CYCLING IN THE LAKE DISTRICT – John Wood *(£7.95)*

LAKELAND ROCKY RAMBLES: Geology beneath your feet – **Brian Lynas** *(£7.95)*

PUB WALKS IN THE LAKE DISTRICT – **Neil Coates** *(£6.95)*

A LOG BOOK OF WAINWRIGHT'S FELLS – **Mark Woosey** *(£7.95)*

WESTERN LAKELAND RAMBLES – **Gordon Brown** *(£5.95)*

LAKELAND WALKING, ON THE LEVEL – **Norman Buckley** *(£6.95)*

MOSTLY DOWNHILL:
LEISURELY WALKS IN THE LAKE DISTRICT – **Alan Pears** *(£6.95)*

THE THIRLMERE WAY – Tim Cappelli *(£6.95)*

THE FURNESS TRAIL – Tim Cappelli *(£6.95)*

CHALLENGING WALKS IN NORTH-WEST BRITAIN – **Ron Astley** *(£9.95)*

We have a wide selection of guides to individual towns, plus outdoor activities centred on walking and cycling in the great outdoors throughout England and Wales. This is a recent selection:

Cycling . . .

CYCLE UK! The essential guide to leisure cycling
– Les Lumsdon *(£9.95)*

OFF-BEAT CYCLING & MOUNTAIN BIKING IN THE PEAK DISTRICT
– Clive Smith *(£6.95)*

MORE OFF-BEAT CYCLING IN THE PEAK DISTRICT – **Clive Smith** *(£6.95)*

50 BEST CYCLE RIDES IN CHESHIRE – edited by **Graham Beech** *(£7.95)*

CYCLING IN THE COTSWOLDS – **Stephen Hill** *(£6.95)*

CYCLING IN THE CHILTERNS – **Henry Tindell** *(£7.95)*

CYCLING IN SOUTH WALES – **Rosemary Evans** *(£7.95)*

CYCLING IN LINCOLNSHIRE – **Penny & Bill Howe** *(£7.95)*

CYCLING IN NORTH STAFFORDSHIRE – **Linda Wain** *(£7.95)*

BY-WAY TRAVELS SOUTH OF LONDON – **Geoff Marshall** *(£7.95)*

Country Walking . . .

FIFTY CLASSIC WALKS IN THE PENNINES – Terry Marsh *(£7.95)*

RAMBLES IN NORTH WALES – Roger Redfern

HERITAGE WALKS IN THE PEAK DISTRICT – Clive Price

EAST CHESHIRE WALKS – Graham Beech

WEST CHESHIRE WALKS – Jen Darling

WEST PENNINE WALKS – Mike Cresswell

NEWARK AND SHERWOOD RAMBLES – Malcolm McKenzie *(£5.95)*

RAMBLES AROUND NOTTINGHAM & DERBY – Keith Taylor

RAMBLES AROUND MANCHESTER – Mike Cresswell

WELSH WALKS: Dolgellau /Cambrian Coast – L. Main & M. Perrott *(£5.95)*

WELSH WALKS: Aberystwyth & District – L. Main & M. Perrott *(£5.95)*

– all of these books are currently £6.95 each, except where indicated

Long-distance walking . . .

WHARFEDALE TO WESTMORLAND:
Historical Walks in the Yorkshire Dales – Aline Watson

THE MARCHES WAY – Les Lumsdon

THE TWO ROSES WAY – Peter Billington *et al*

THE RED ROSE WAY – Tom Schofield

– all £6.95 each

Pub Walks . . .

A fabulous series of 'Pub Walks' books for just about every popular walking area in the UK, all featuring access by public transport • A new series of investigations into the Supernatural • Superb illustrated books on Manchester's football teams

– plus many more entertaining and educational books being regularly added to our list. All of our books are available from your local bookshop. In case of difficulty, or to obtain our complete catalogue, please contact:

Sigma Leisure, 1 South Oak Lane, Wilmslow, Cheshire SK9 6AR

Phone: 0625 – 531035   Fax: 0625 – 536800

ACCESS and VISA orders welcome – call our friendly sales staff or use our 24 hour Answerphone service! Most orders are despatched on the day we receive your order – you could be enjoying our books in just a couple of days.